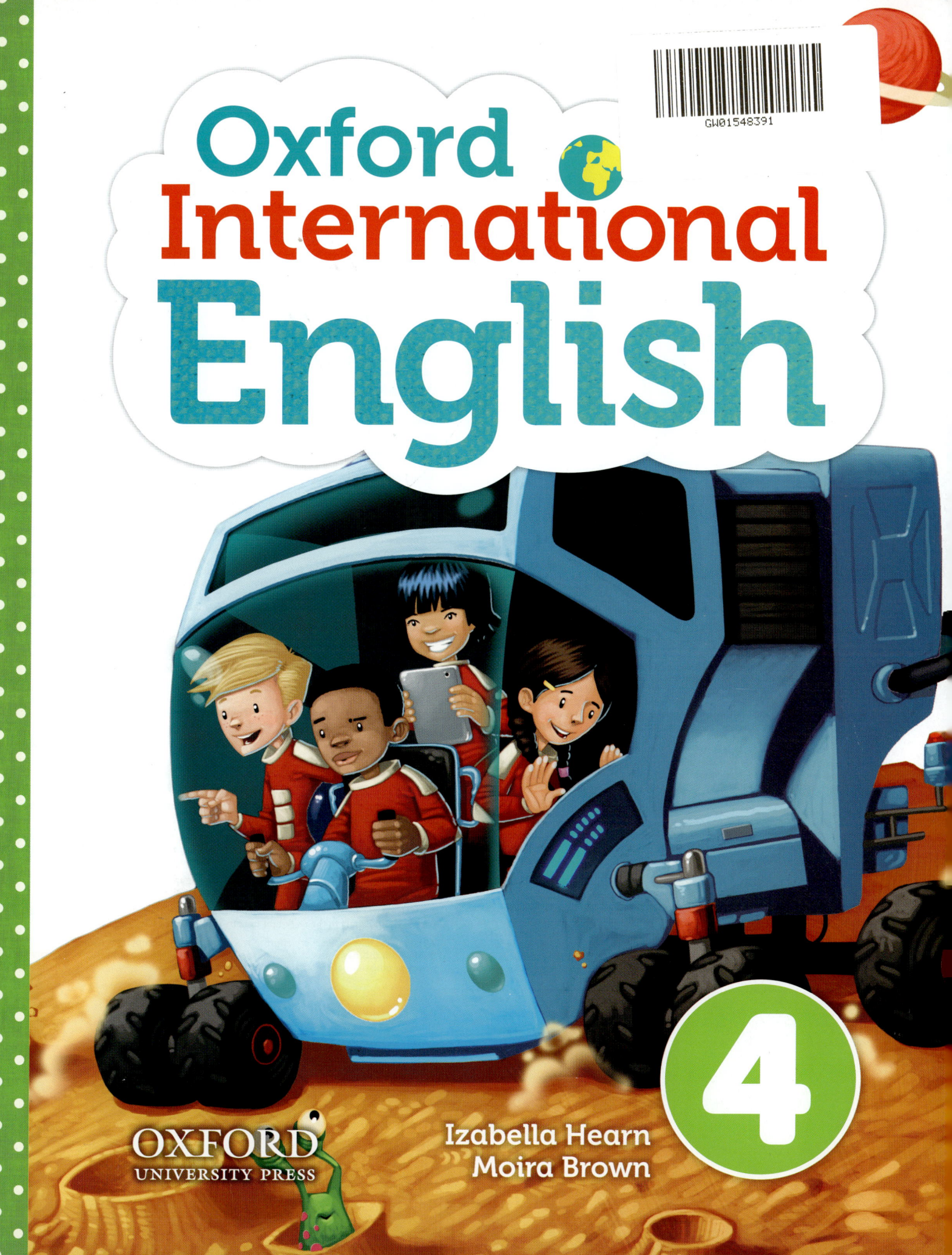

Great Clarendon Street, Oxford OX2 6DP

Oxford University Press is a department of the University of Oxford.
It furthers the University's objective of excellence in research, scholarship,
and education by publishing worldwide in

© Oxford University Press

The moral rights of the authors have been asserted.

First published 2013

All rights reserved. No part of this publication may be reproduced, stored in a retrieval system, or transmitted, in any form or by any means, without the prior permission in writing of Oxford University Press, or as expressly permitted by law, by licence or under terms agreed with the appropriate reprographics rights organization. Enquiries concerning reproduction outside the scope of the above should be sent to the Rights Department, Oxford University Press, at the address above.

You must not circulate this work in any other form and you must impose this same condition on any acquirer.

British Library Cataloguing in Publication Data
Data available

ISBN- 978-019-839034-3

20 19 18 17 16 15 14

Printed in India by Manipal Technologies Limited

Paper used in the production of this book is a natural, recyclable product made from wood grown in sustainable forests. The manufacturing process conforms to the environmental regulations of the country of origin.

Acknowledgements

Cover illustration: Andy Elkerton

Illustrations are by: Mark Braught, Patricia Castelao, Pippa Curnick, Evelyne Duverne, Dave Hill, Milena Jahier, Richard Morgan, Sole Otero, Dusan Pavlic, Marcin Pinowarski, Martin Remphry, Iva Sasheva, Graham Smith, Michael Terry, Claudia Venturini.

The publishers would like to thank the following for permissions to use their photographs:

p8: Bridgeman/School is Out, 1889, Forbes, Elizabeth Adela Stanhope (1859-1912)/© Penlee House Gallery and Museum, Penzance, Cornwall, UK/The Bridgeman Art Library; p8 (frame): Shutterstock/ nodff; p8 (easel): Shutterstock/ AR Images; p9tr: Shutterstock/VICTOR TORRES; p9cr: Shutterstock/luca85; p9br: Shutterstock/de2marco; p9bc: Shutterstock/Thomas Bethge; p9bl: Shutterstock/chippix; p11: Shutterstock/Thomas Bethge; p13: Shutterstock; p15: Shutterstock/Madlen; p16: istockphoto/deezaat; p17: istockphoto/digitalskillet; p18: Shutterstock/PHOTOCREO Michal Bednarek; p19: Shutterstock/Vidux; p24tl: OUP/Photodisc; p24tr: Shutterstock/irin-k; p24cl: Shutterstock/chanwangrong; p24cr: Shutterstock/Shachar Weis; p24bl: Shutterstock/Zheltyshev; p24br: Shutterstock/irin-k; p25: Shutterstock/StudioSmart; p27b: Corbis/© Pierre Holtz/Reuters/Corbis; p28t: OUP/Corbis; p28bl: Shutterstock/Marco Uliana; p28br: Shutterstock/Mircea BEZERGHEANU; p29t: Shutterstock/Julien Tromeur; p29b: OUP/Niamh Baldock; p31: Shutterstock/Subbotina Anna; p32: Shutterstock/Jacob Hamblin; p33: Shutterstock/nagib; p34: Shutterstock/Fer Gregory; p38: Corbis/© Martin Gallagher/Corbis; p39: Shutterstock/Matthew Cole; p40t: Corbis/© Ocean/Corbis; p40c: Alamy/© Greg Balfour Evans/Alamy; p40 (background): Shutterstock/Repina Valeriya; p41: Shutterstock/Daniel Wiedemann; p45: Corbis/© Serge Kozak/Corbis; p48: Shutterstock/Clipart Corner; p53: Shutterstock/Mumut; p54 (background): Shutterstock/Dimales; p54 (background): Shutterstock/Bertold Werkmann; p55: Shutterstock/Bob Orsillo; p58: Shutterstock/Pius Lee; p61: Shutterstock/Jacek Chabraszewski; p64: Shutterstock/Jaren Jai Wicklund; p70tl: Shutterstock/Mirek Srb; p70bl: Shutterstock/davemhuntphotography; p70r: Shutterstock/Jiri Haurelijuk; p71: Shutterstock/Willyam Bradberry; p72: Shutterstock/Elena Larina; p73: Shutterstock/Willyam Bradberry; p75: Corbis/© David Deas/DK Stock/Corbis; p76: Associated Press/Achmad Ibrahim/AP/Press Association Images; p77: Shutterstock/Jennifer Stone; p80: Shutterstock/Virinaflora; p81: Shutterstock/Elena Elisseeva; p83: Shutterstock/Jason Winter; p86 (background): Shutterstock/dedoma; p86tr: istockphoto/hadynyah; p86cl: istockphoto/brittak; p86br: istockphoto/hadynyah; p87: Shutterstock/defpicture; p93: Alamy/© Jake Lyell/Alamy; p94: Shutterstock/irabel8; p96t: Shutterstock/LeventeGyori; p96b: Shutterstock/Diego Cervo; p97t: Alamy/© Blue Jean Images/Alamy; p97b: Alamy/© Image Source/Alamy; P99: Shutterstock/Villiers Steyn; p100: Corbis/© Philippe Lissac/Godong/Corbis; p101t: Shutterstock/Tatyana Vyc; p101b: Shutterstock/Sergey Novikov; p105: Shutterstock/STILLFX; p107: Shutterstock/Molodec; p109: Corbis/© Floresco Productions/Corbis; p111: Shutterstock/gasa; p114: Corbis/© Caroline Penn/CORBIS; p116l: Bridgeman/Mama (oil on canvas), Willis, Tilly (Contemporary Artist)/Private Collection/The Bridgeman Art Library; p116r: Bridgeman/The Water Hole (w/c on paper), Wood, Stanley L. (1866-1928)/Private Collection/Peter Newark Western Americana/The Bridgeman Art Library; p117t: Corbis/© SUKREE SUKPLANG/Reuters/Corbis; p117b: Shutterstock/topten22photo/Shutterstock.com; p118t: Shutterstock/kurhan; p118b: Shutterstock/africa924/Shutterstock.com; p119: Corbis/© James Marshall/Corbis; p121: Shutterstock/Lovingyou2911/Shutterstock.com; p122: Shutterstock/Pakhnyushcha; p123: Shutterstock/Creative Travel Projects; p124: Shutterstock/stockshoppe; p127: Corbis/© Gideon Mendel/In Pictures/Corbis; p128: Shutterstock/Merkushev Vasiliy; p129: Shutterstock/Vasaleks; p130t: Shutterstock/Matthew Cole; p130b: Shutterstock/Olympus; p131: Shutterstock/HitToon.Com; p132l: Shutterstock/Ambient Ideas; p132r: Shutterstock/Samot; p133: Shutterstock/Happy person; p136: Shutterstock/olies; p138: Shutterstock/Welena; p139: Shutterstock/Tom Bird; p141t: Shutterstock/tassel78; p142: Corbis/© Stephanie Rabemiafara/Art in All of Us/Corbis; p143: Shutterstock/Kudryashka.

The author and publisher are grateful for permission to reprint the following copyright material:

Donna Bailey: *Wasting Water (What We Can Do)* (Franklin Watts, 1991), reprinted by permission of the publishers, Franklin Watts, an imprint of Hachette Children's Books.

Matsuo Basho: Haiku, translated by *Harry Behn from Cricket Songs: Japanese Haiku* (Houghton Mifflin, 1964), reprinted by permission of Curtis Brown Ltd, New York on behalf of the Estate of Harry Behn.

Alison Chisholm: 'Riddle', copyright © Alison Chisholm 2007, first published in *Poems about Earth* compiled by Andrew Fusek Peters (Evans, 2007), reprinted by permission of the author.

Vassilis Comporozos: 'Yellow Leaves', published at www.poetrysoup.com, reprinted by permission of the author.

Julia Donaldson: 'The Wonderful Smells' from *Play Time* (Macmillan Children's Books, 2013), first published in *Reading 360: Plays: The Wonderful Smells*, (Ginn, 1996), copyright © Julia Donaldson 1996, reprinted by permission of Pearson Education Ltd.

Eva Ibbotson: *The Abominables* (Marion Lloyd Books, 2012), text copyright © Eva Ibbotson 2012, reprinted by permission of Scholastic Ltd. All rights reserved.

Mike Jubb: 'Word Journey', copyright © Mike Jubb 2013, reprinted from his website by permission of the author.

Kids National Geographic: 'Who's the fastest jaw on the draw?' and 'Sea Turtle Soup? No thanks' by Catherine Clarke Fox; 'Giant panda cubs give hope to an endangered species' by David George Gordon; 'The Secret Language of Dolphins' by NGS staff writer; and 'Tigers Cuddle with Apes' by Aline Alexander Newman, all from www.kids.nationalgeographic.com, copyright © NGS, reprinted by permission of National Geographic Stock.

John Kitching: 'History', first published in *The Works 2* chosen by Brian Moses and Pie Corbett (Macmillan Children's Books, 2002), reprinted by permission of the author.

Matt Minshall: *What Can You See in This Cloud?* (Treetops Non-Fiction, OUP, 2005), copyright © Matt Minshall 2005, reprinted by permission of Oxford University Press.

Naomi Shibab Nye: *Sitti's Secrets* (Hamish Hamilton, 1994), text copyright © Naomi Shibab Nye 1994, by permission of Penguin Books Ltd and Simon & Schuster Books for Young Readers, an imprint of Simon & Schuster Children's Publishing Division.

UNICEF: *A Life Like Mine: How Children Live Around the World* (DK in association with UNICEF, 2002), copyright © Dorling Kindersley Ltd 2002, reprinted by permission of Dorling Kindersley Ltd, London.

Margaret Walker: 'Lineage' from *This is My Century: New and Collected Poems* (University of Georgia Press, 1989), reprinted by permission of the publishers

Kathryn White: *Carving the Sea Path* (Evans, 2009), reprinted by permission of the author c/o Rogers Coleridge & White, 20 Powis Mews, London W11 1JN.

Janet Wong: 'Tea Ceremony' from *A Suitcase of Seaweed and Other Poems* (Booksurge (self) Publishing, 2008) and 'Good Luck Gold' from Good Luck Gold and *Other Poems* (CreateSpace Independent Publishing, 2012), reprinted by permission of the author.

Penelope York: *BUGS* (DK Eyewonder, 2005), copyright © Dorling Kindersley Ltd 2002, reprinted by permission of Dorling Kindersley Ltd, London

Any third party use of this material, outside of this publication, is prohibited. Interested parties should apply to the copyright holders indicated in each case.

Although we have made every effort to trace and contact all copyright holders before publication this has not been possible in all cases. If notified, the publisher will rectify any errors or omissions at the earliest opportunity.

Contents

A world of stories, poems and facts 4
Unit contents 6

1 Life long ago 8

2 Beautiful bugs! 24

3 Tricks and truth 40

Revise and check 1 52

4 Fantastic journeys 54

5 Amazing animals 70

6 Families of the world 86

Revise and check 2 98

7 All together! 100

8 World of water 116

9 Poems for all seasons 132

Revise and check 3 144

Reading fiction 146
Carving the Sea Path

A world of stories, poems and facts

Unit contents

Unit	Theme	Reading and comprehension
1	Life long ago	**Fiction** Narrative with an historical setting *Anne of Green Gables*
2	Beautiful bugs!	**Non-fiction** Non-chronological report *Bugs*
3	Tricks and truth	**Play script** A play on a common theme *The Wonderful Smells*
		REVISE AND CHECK UNITS 1–3
4	Fantastic journeys	**Fiction** Fantasy narrative *The Abominables*
5	Amazing animals	**Non-fiction** Newspaper-style reports *The Secret Language of Dolphins*, *Tigers Cuddle with Apes*
6	Families of the world	**Poetry** Poems from different times and cultures *Good Luck Gold*, *Tea Ceremony*, *Lineage*
		REVISE AND CHECK UNITS 4–6
7	All together!	**Fiction** Narrative about problems and issues *Sitti's Secrets*
8	World of water	**Non-fiction** Persuasive and explanatory texts *What We Can Do About Wasting Water*, *What Can You See in This Cloud?*
9	Poems for all seasons	**Poetry** Different forms of poems *Haiku*, *Tanka (Yellow Leaves)*, *Cinquain (Snow)*, *Shape poem (Sun)*, *List poem (Spring is in the Air)*, *Riddle*, *Limerick (There was an Old Man in a Tree)*
		REVISE AND CHECK UNITS 7–9
		FICTION READING *Carving the Sea Path*

Language, grammar, spelling, vocabulary, phonics, punctuation	Writing	Speaking and listening
• Unfamiliar words, definitions • Adverbs and adverbial phrases • Verbs and tenses, *past*, *present and future* • Irregular verbs, *to be*, *to have* • Clauses and commas • Features of fiction genre	Fiction Writing an historical story	Language choices Expressing opinions
• New words in context • Prefixes and suffixes, *un-*, *dis-*, *re-*, *-hood*, *-ship*, *-ness*, *-al-* • Adverbs, the suffix *-ly* • Punctuation marks • Alphabetical order • Dictionary use and extension of vocabulary • Features of non-chronological reports	Non-fiction Planning and writing a non-chronological report	Expressing opinions Confident talking in discussion
• Unfamiliar words, definitions • Irregular verbs and the past tense • Powerful verbs • Features of play scripts	Play script Completing a play script on a common theme	Questions – develop ideas and extend understanding Play script performance
• Unfamiliar words, definitions • Apostrophes and contractions • Apostrophes and possession • Plurals, adding -s • Similes • Features of fantasy stories	Fiction Writing a beginning to a fantasy story	Expressing opinions Confident talking in discussion
• New words in context • Apostrophes – plurals and possession • Metaphors • Adjectives – comparative and superlative • Adjectives of intensity • Features of newspaper-style reports	Non-fiction Writing a newspaper-style report	Language choices Organization of ideas
• Unfamiliar words, definitions • Figurative language, simile and metaphor • Alliteration and rhyme • Poetic imagery and language • Features of poetry genre	Poetry Writing a poem using a model	Expressing opinions Questions – ideas and understanding Poetry performance
• New words in context • Homophones • Different types of sentences • Character description • Features of fiction genre	Fiction Writing a story with an everyday setting	Expressing opinions Organization of ideas
• Unfamiliar words, definitions • Connectives in sentences • Words with common roots • Features of persuasive texts • Features of explanatory texts	Non-fiction Planning and writing an explanatory text	Organization of ideas Language choices
• Unfamiliar words, definitions • Same letter, different sound • Alliteration and personification • Imagery and rhyme • Syllabic patterns in poetry • Features of poetry genre	Poetry Writing a poem	Poetry performance Language choices Confident talking in discussion

Fiction Speaking and listening

1 Life long ago

"History
Is also your small
yesterday and mine."
John Kitching

Let's Talk

1 Look at this painting of a classroom. How do you know it is from long ago?
2 How does the painting make you feel?

Fiction Speaking, listening and vocabulary

Using words

Word Cloud
centuries
decade
laws

A Look at the words in the Word Cloud and match them to the meanings here.

1 Units of time of one hundred years.
2 Rules that people in a society have to follow.
3 A period of ten years.

B Anne is describing her school. Look at the pictures and use the correct words to fill the gaps.

Today is September 20th, 1908. Today, I'm going to use my _____ to write some sums on my _____ . I sometimes use the _____ to help me count, too. Then the teacher writes the answers on the _____ for us.

blackboard

abacus

C This is Anne's classroom. Does it look like yours? Work with a partner and name three things that are different from your classroom. Use the pictures on this page to help you.

chalk

slate

Fiction Reading

Historical fiction

This story takes place in Canada in 1908. Anne is an eleven-year-old orphan, who has been adopted by Marilla and Matthew Cuthbert. Anne is delighted by her new home at Green Gables and her new friends and school in Avonlea.

Word Cloud
dictation
disgraceful
imagination
scrumptious

Anne's First Day

The Avonlea school was a whitewashed building with big windows. It was furnished with comfortable, old-fashioned desks that opened and shut. Over the years, generations of
5 school children had carved their initials onto the wooden lids. Behind the schoolhouse was a brook where all the children put their bottles of milk to keep them cool and sweet until dinner hour.

Marilla felt worried when she first sent
10 Anne to school. Anne was such an odd girl. How was she going to get on with the other children? And was she going to manage to keep quiet during her lessons? But things went better than Marilla had
15 hoped. Anne came home that evening full of happy chatter.

Fiction Reading

"I think I like school here," she announced. "I didn't really like Mr Phillips, the master, though."

"Anne, I don't want to hear you talking 20 about your teacher like that," said Marilla, sharply. "I hope you were a good girl."

"Of course I was," said Anne. "And I didn't even have to try hard to be good. I had scrumptious fun playing outside, but I'm 25 dreadfully far behind the others in lessons. Though no one has an imagination like mine. We had reading and geography and Canadian history and dictation today. Mr Phillips said my spelling 30 was disgraceful and he held up my slate so everyone could see it. I was so embarrassed!"

Adapted from the original *Anne of Green Gables*, by L. M. Montgomery

Glossary

generations
a single part of a family; the children, or the parents

initials
the first letter of a person's first name and surname/s

whitewashed
covered with a white liquid, like paint

Comprehension

 **Read and answer the questions.**

1. Find a phrase in the story to describe the school in Avonlea.
2. Find the parts of the text that tell us why Marilla was worried about sending Anne to school.
3. What lessons did Anne have on her first day at school?
4. We know that the story takes place in the past. Find a sentence that tells us this is not modern day.

Fiction Comprehension

What do you think?
Use phrases from the story to help with your answers.
1. How does Anne feel about her new school?
2. Why do you think she might not like the master?
3. Why do you think Anne might need to 'try hard' to be good?
4. How do you feel towards Anne? Is she different to a modern character?

What about you?
How would you feel about going to a new school? Would it be scary or would it be an adventure?

Discussion time
Anne felt nervous about her first day in her new school. Discuss what would be the best five pieces of advice to give a new student arriving in your class or school for the first time.

Historical fiction (continued)

An Angry Incident

Word Cloud
algebra
dreamland
passionately
snooty

The Avonlea school had just one class, which was full of children of all ages. Mr Phillips was helping Prissy with her algebra. The others were doing whatever
5 they liked – eating green apples, whispering, drawing pictures on their slates, and playing with crickets that they had caught from the fields. Gilbert Blythe was a handsome boy with curly brown hair and a twinkle in his eyes. He
10 was trying to make Anne look at him but Anne was busy daydreaming. She was gazing out of the window at the shimmering blue water of the lake. She was far away in a gorgeous dreamland and could not hear or see anything
15 around her.

Gilbert Blythe was used to getting his own way. That snooty red-haired Anne girl with big eyes *should* look at him.

Gilbert reached over and picked
20 up the end of Anne's long red plait. He held it up and whispered loudly:

"Carrots! Carrots!"

Anne looked at Gilbert fiercely. She jumped to her feet in a rage.

25 "You mean and hateful boy!" she cried passionately. "How dare you!"

Adapted from the original *Anne of Green Gables*, by L. M. Montgomery

Fiction Comprehension

Comprehension

A Which three sentences below are true?

1 The children were drawing on their slates.
2 Gilbert wanted Anne to look at him.
3 Anne was concentrating on her work.
4 Anne was cross with Gilbert.

B **What do you think?**

Use phrases from the story to help with your answers.

1 Are the children in the Avonlea class well-behaved? Find three examples in the story.
2 How do we know that Anne was not interested in the lesson?
3 What phrases in the story tell us that Gilbert is a confident boy?

Challenge
Notice how the story is introduced, then builds in excitement. What do you think might happen next? Make up your own ending for the story.

C **What about you?**

Anne is very upset about Gilbert calling her 'Carrots'. Have you ever felt so angry? Do you think Anne was right to be so cross with Gilbert?

Fiction Grammar

Adverbs

Adverbs tell us more about verbs. They make sentences much more interesting.

Adverbs of place tell us **where**.

Example: The children sat **in the Avonlea schoolroom**.

Adverbs of time tell us **when**.

Example: The teacher arrived **late**.

Adverbs of manner tell us **how**.

Example: Anne wrote on her slate **neatly**.

Top Tip

Many adverbs are one word, but some can be a phrase of two or three words. *Example*: **in the park**, or **last night**. These are adverbial phrases.

A Look at the bold words in these sentences. What kind of adverbs are they? Do they answer the question where, when, or how?

1 Anne went for a picnic **in the orchard**.
2 It was a lovely day and the sun was shining **brightly**.
3 **By lunchtime**, Anne was feeling hungry.

B Find one example of each kind of adverb in the story on pages 10, 11 and 14.

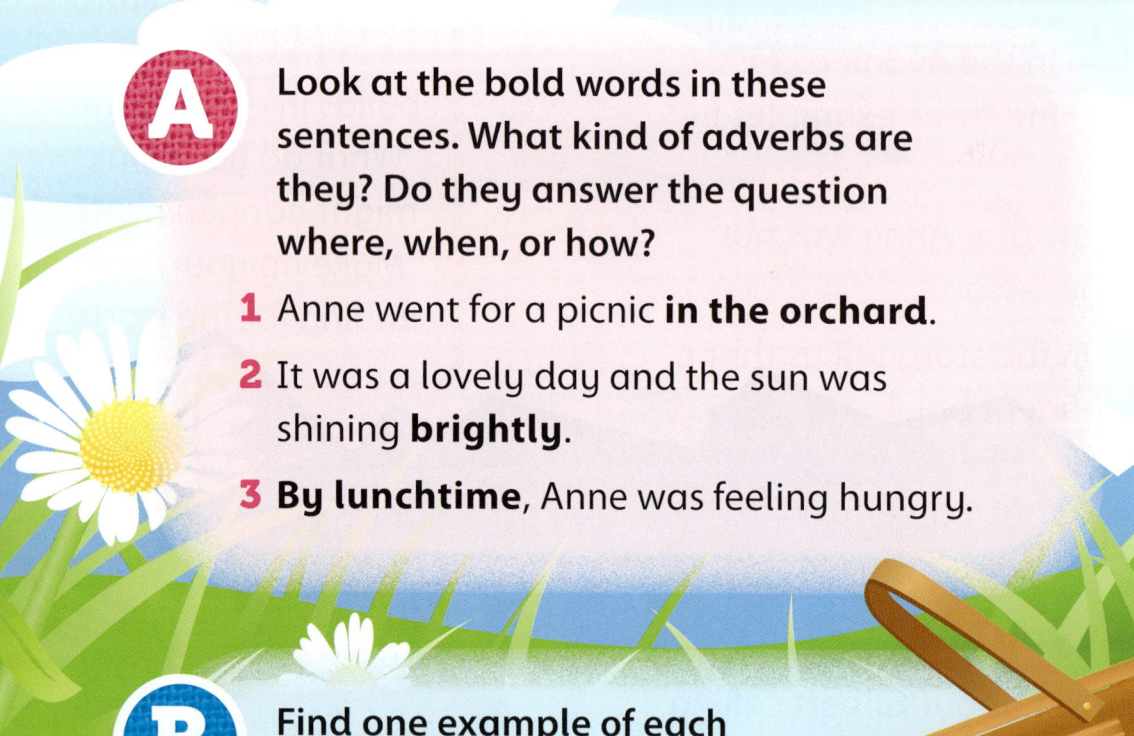

Fiction Grammar

Verbs and tenses

 **A** Look at the verbs below. They are different parts of the irregular verbs 'to be' and 'to have'.

was had is am have being are has were having

1 Make a list of all of the parts that belong to the verb 'to be'.
2 Make a list of all of the parts that belong to the verb 'to have'.

To be
I am
You are
He/She is
We are
You are
They are

To have
I have
You have
He/She has
We have
You have
They have

B Look at Anne's story on pages 10, 11 and 14.

1 Find examples of sentences in the present, past and future tenses.
2 Look at the verbs. Are they all regular?

Remember: Some verbs are **irregular verbs**. This means they do not follow the usual pattern when we use them in different tenses. *Example:* the verb **to go**:

In the **present** tense: They **go** to the beach every summer. In the **past tense**: Yesterday, they **went** on a trip to the beach.

Fiction Grammar

Clauses

Sentences are made of clauses. All clauses have a **verb**.

A **main clause** can make sense on its own.
Example: Anne and Diana **enjoyed** the day.

A **subordinate clause** must be added to a main clause. It doesn't make sense on its own.
Example: because they **played** in the meadow.

Together, the **main clause** and the **subordinate clause** make sense:

Anne and Diana **enjoyed** the day, because they **played** in the meadow.

Top Tip

A subordinate clause adds information to the main clause of the sentence.

A Copy out these sentences and underline the main clauses.
1 At the weekends, the children liked to play outside.
2 In the holidays, when the weather is sunny, the family like to go to the seaside.

B Look at the sentence below. It has a main clause and a subordinate clause. The main clause comes first.

Anne chatted about school, while Marilla made the tea.

Make up three new sentences of your own. Use the same main clause, but change the subordinate clause to something different each time.

Fiction Grammar and punctuation

Commas

Commas (,) are punctuation marks that are used to show a small pause in a sentence.

Sentences with main and subordinate clauses need commas when:

The subordinate clause comes **first**.

Example: **Although it was raining**, Anne went for a walk.

And when the subordinate clause comes **in the middle** of a main clause.

Example: The school, **which was painted white**, had big windows.

Look for the main and subordinate clauses in these sentences. Add in the commas where they are needed.

1 As there were no pens children used chalk to write on their slates.
2 The children who were being naughty played with crickets in the classroom.

Add the subordinate clauses in brackets into the sentences. Make sure you put commas in the right places.

1 The classroom was full of children. (which was quite small)
2 Gilbert liked to tease the girls. (who was a handsome boy)

Fiction Writing workshop

Writing an historical story
Model writing

Abandoned

Albert Jones, a small, thin boy with an anxious face, was struggling to carry a large bucket of water upstairs for his mistress's bath. He sighed. The household chores had been so hard this morning!

"Be careful, boy. You're going to spill it!" The harsh screech of the housekeeper's voice made Albert stumble, the bucket of water slipping from his hands. In dismay, Albert watched the water cascade down the stairs…

"Sorry. I was just…"

The housekeeper leapt forward, her lips curled in a sneer, "Just! After all the Smith family have done for you. Giving you a job after your good for nothing parents decided to emigrate to Canada and then not come back."

It was then that Albert decided to cry…

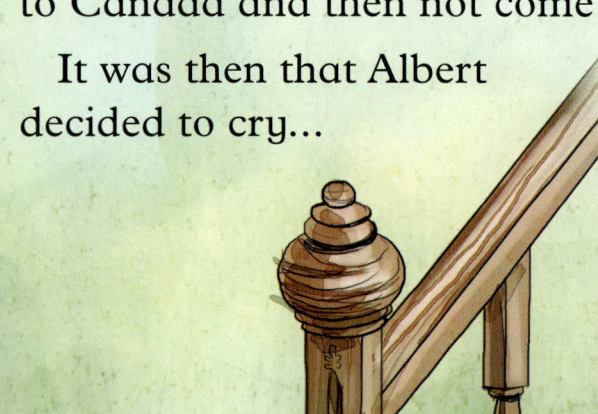

Fiction Writing workshop

Guided writing

Getting started!

In your story, the first two paragraphs introduce the characters and the setting.

Characters Give clues about the characters – what they look like, how they move and speak, and what they say.	Albert – small, thin, weak, tearful. Housekeeper – screeching voice, sneering, strict and cruel to Albert. A bully!
Setting Give clues about where and when it's taking place.	Large house. America in 1900s – young boy as servant and housekeepers were normal. No modern plumbing or hot water.

You will need to make your readers want to read more. Build some excitement and create some problems so that your readers will want to see what happens.

Example: Will the housekeeper continue to be cruel to Albert? Will his parents come back?

Fiction Writing workshop

Writing an historical story
Your writing

Carry on writing the story of Albert and write four more paragraphs. Use the paragraph plan below to help you write your story. The topic sentence is the sentence you need to give more detail about in each paragraph. You can use the ones here or you can use your own.

1	Things get worse for Albert.	*Today, everything went wrong for Albert.*
2	The problems build the excitement.	*Things just seemed to get worse and worse.*
3	The problems are sorted out.	*Mrs Smith was extremely cross about the behaviour of the housekeeper.*
4	The conclusion brings the story to an end.	*Albert couldn't believe it when he opened the door and saw his parents standing there.*

Fiction Writing workshop

Historical fiction success criteria

When you are writing your story, remember to think about success criteria. This is the list of skills you need to show. Draw a chart of your own, like the one below, and put ticks in the boxes. Check and edit your work as you go along.

	Yes	No	Sometimes
Story develops through: build up of problems / solving problems / conclusion	✓		
Each paragraph is written from a topic sentence		✓	
Clues are given about historical characters and setting	✓		
Characters are shown through what they look like and say	✓		
Past, present and future tense verbs used			
Some subordinate clauses used (sometimes with commas)			
Full stops and capital letters used properly			
Spelling correct	✓		

Read your story aloud to a partner. Ask your partner if they can suggest ways for you to improve your story.

Non-fiction Speaking and listening

2 Beautiful bugs!

"If you want to live and thrive, let the spider run alive!"
Traditional saying

Let's Talk

1 Which bugs and insects are common where you live?
2 Are any of them dangerous? How do you feel about them?

Non-fiction Speaking, listening and vocabulary

Thinking about insects

 Look at the words in the Word Cloud and match them to the meanings here.

1 A group of living things that are similar and can produce young together.
2 Something that is annoying or causes damage.
3 To move pollen to a plant to help the plant make seeds.

Word Cloud
pest
pollinate
species

 Write questions for these answers.

1 Bees are the only insects that make food for humans.
2 Bees are important because they pollinate many plants that we grow for food.
3 Scientists are worried because the number of bees is dropping.

 Do you think bugs and insects are important – or are they just pests? Discuss your ideas with a partner.

Non-fiction Reading

Non-chronological reports

Bugs

Word Cloud
amber
damage
skeleton

Bugs, bugs, bugs
Most of the bugs that you know are called arthropods, which means they have their skeleton on the outside of their bodies. There
5 are over a million known species of arthropods on the Earth…

We know that insects were around over 40 million years ago because some were trapped in a substance called amber,
10 which hardened back then.

What is an insect?
You can spot an insect by counting its body parts and legs. They all have
15 six legs and three body parts – a head, a thorax, and an abdomen.

What is a myriapod?
If you try counting the legs on a
20 creepy crawly and you find you can't, the chances are you are looking at a myriapod, such as a millipede or centipede. They have
25 lots of segments and lots and lots of legs!

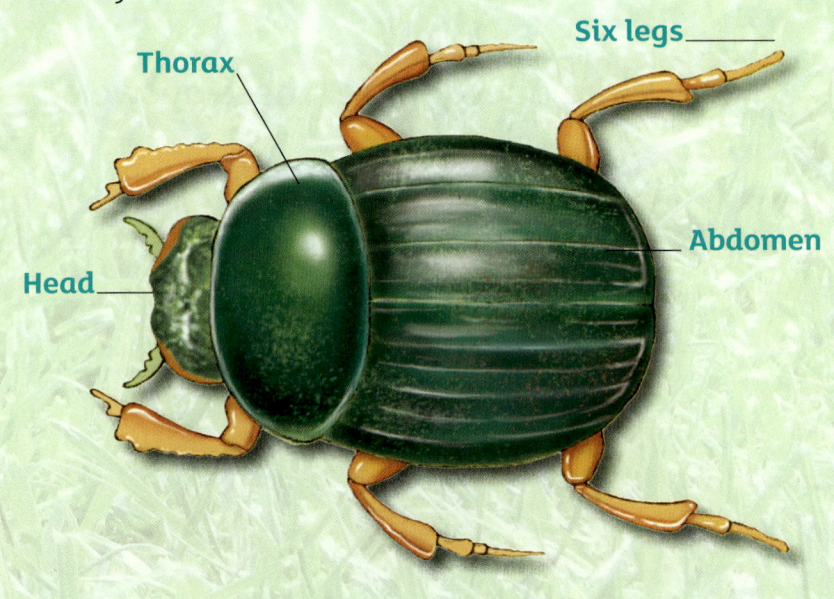

Not all myriapods have the same number of segments and legs. Centipedes can have from 15 pairs of legs to as many as 171 pairs!

Non-fiction Reading

What is an arachnid?
All arachnids have eight legs. Watch out however, other than
30 spiders, a lot of arachnids look like insects so count carefully.

What is a true bug?
These days we tend to call all creepy crawlies 'bugs'… But
35 actually a true bug is a type of insect that has a long mouthpart that it pierces its food with, then uses it to suck up the inside of the food…

Pests and plagues
40 They may be small but bugs can do a surprising amount of damage – in large numbers or on their own. Us humans sometimes have to try hard to control them, and very often we lose.

From DK Eyewonder *Bugs*, by Penelope York

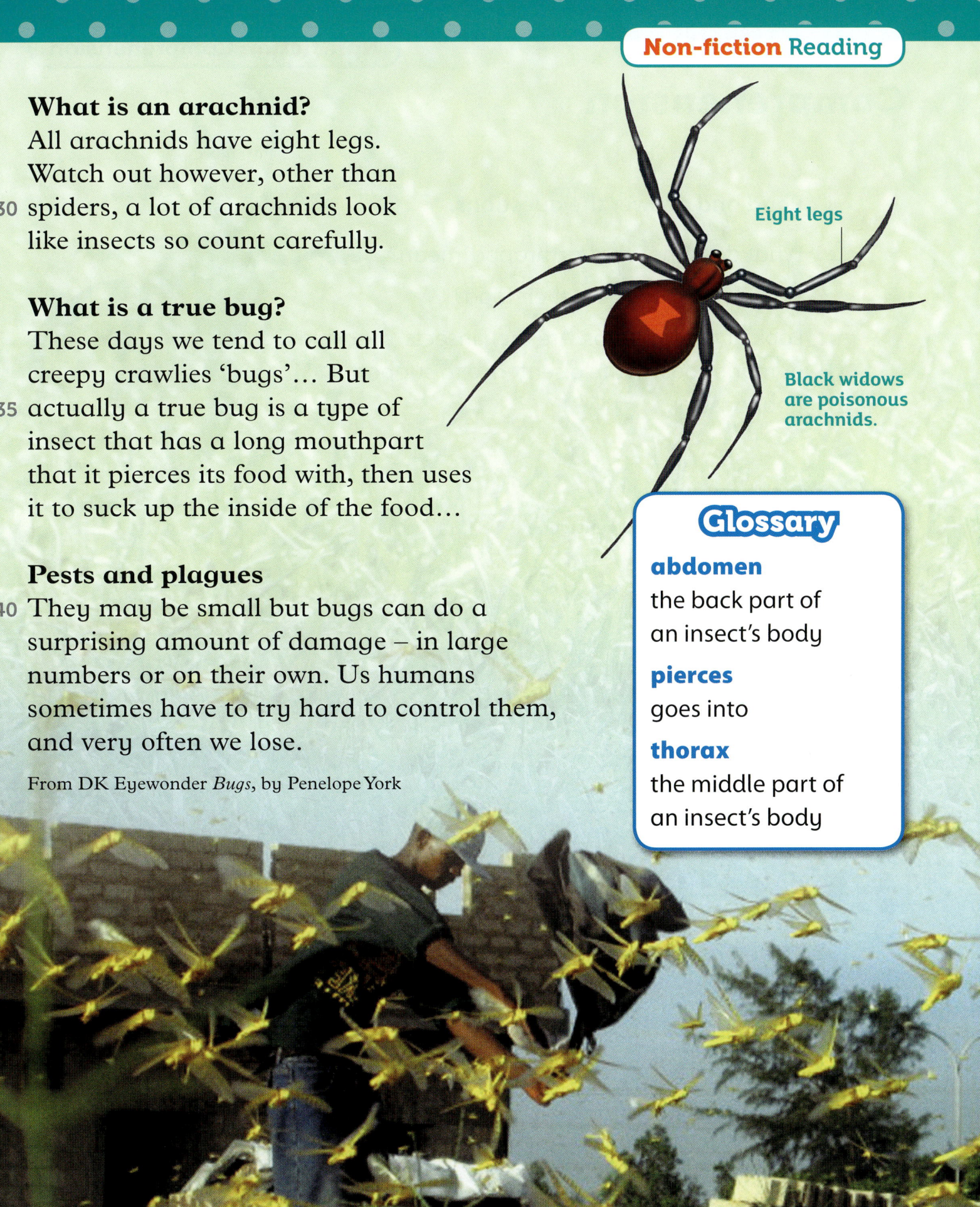

Eight legs

Black widows are poisonous arachnids.

Glossary

abdomen
the back part of an insect's body

pierces
goes into

thorax
the middle part of an insect's body

Non-fiction Comprehension

Comprehension

A Read and answer the questions.

1 What does the word 'arthropod' mean?
2 How do true bugs eat their food?
3 Look at these photos. Are they insects, arachnids or myriapods? Write a sentence to support your answer.

Frog-legged leaf beetle

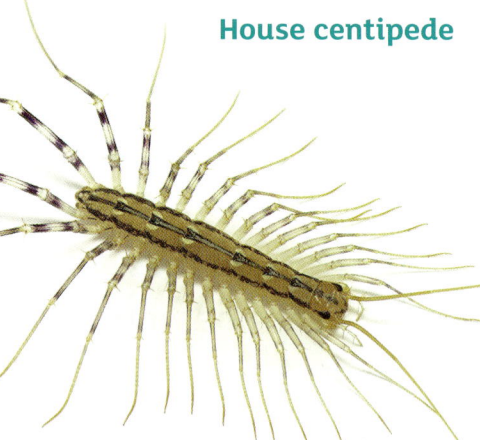
House centipede

Male ladybird spider

B What do you think?

1 The extract is organized into paragraphs. Why do you think this is?
2 Many of the paragraphs have a question as a heading. What question could you give as a title to the whole extract?
3 Which tense are most of the sentences written in?
4 Read the final paragraph 'Pests and plagues' again. How would you summarize this paragraph in one sentence?

Non-fiction Comprehension

C What about you?

What more would you like to find out about bugs? Think of two questions and then try to find the answers to your questions.

Discussion time

Insects are nutritious and people around the world think they are tasty! In countries such as Thailand, Australia, Brazil and China, it is common to find insects on the menu. Have you eaten a bug before? If not, what do you think one might taste like?

Non-fiction Reading

Non-chronological reports (continued)

Bugs

Water world
If you find a body of water, the chances are it's filled with mini-life – but you may have to look closely to see some of it. Many
5   bugs live in or above the water and some can even walk on the surface.

Diving in
The diving beetle is the great meat eater of the water. It tucks a bubble of air under its wings so
10 it can breathe underwater, and dives down to catch tadpoles and even small fish.

Walking on water
Pond skaters can walk on water because of thick, waterproof hairs on their feet. They skim
15 over the surface looking for floating food.

Darting around
The beautiful dragonfly lives above water. It is called the dragonfly because of its very aggressive 'dragon-like' behaviour.

From DK Eyewonder *Bugs*, by Penelope York

Word Cloud
aggressive
surface
waterproof

Comprehension

Non-fiction Comprehension

Explain the following phrases in your own words.

1 a body of water
2 skim over the surface
3 'dragon-like' behaviour

What do you think?

1 How do the subheadings give us an idea of the information in each paragraph? Give two examples.
2 A **topic sentence** introduces the subject. Where does it come in the paragraph?
3 Do you think the sentences in the extract are written in a formal or an informal (chatty) style?

Discussion time

Some people say that they behave in a way that respects nature. What do you think this means? Do you try to behave this way?

What about you?

Research another water bug. Write a topic sentence and then add some detail. What subheading will you give your paragraph?

Non-fiction Grammar

Prefixes and suffixes

A **prefix** is a group of letters we put in front of a word.
A **suffix** is a group of letters we put at the end of a word.
Prefixes and suffixes change the meaning of the word.
Example: **dis** + appear = disappear (**dis** is the prefix)
child + **hood** = childhood (**hood** is the suffix)

Top Tip

When we add a **prefix** to a word, we sometimes need to add a **hyphen** between them.
Example: re-read

A Choose a suffix to add to these words.

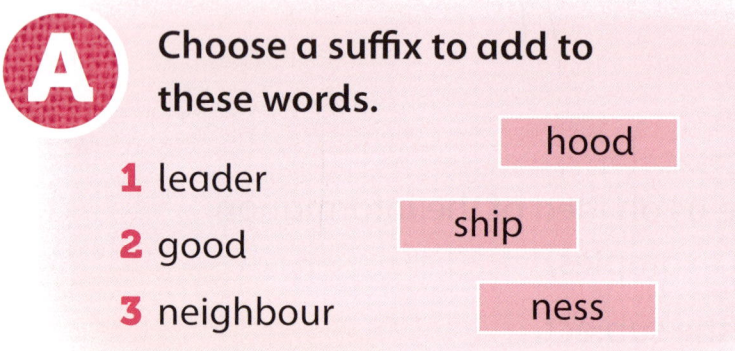

1 leader
2 good
3 neighbour

hood
ship
ness

B Choose a prefix to add to these words.

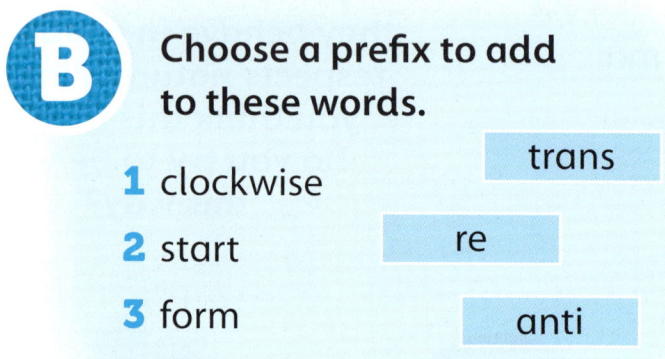

1 clockwise
2 start
3 form

trans
re
anti

C The letters **al** can be used as both a prefix and a suffix. Add **al** to the beginning or the end of these words.

ways   season   most   though   nation   accident   one

Non-fiction Grammar

Adverbs – the suffix –ly

Remember: **Adverbs** tell us more about verbs. Most adverbs of manner are formed by adding the suffix **–ly** to an adjective.

Example: soft – soft**ly**   bad – bad**ly**   correct – correct**ly**

Adjectives that end in a **consonant + y** drop the **y** and take **–ily**.

Example: easy – eas**ily**   happy – happ**ily**

Adjectives that end in **–le** drop the **e** and take **–y**.

Example: simple – simpl**y**   comfortable – comfortabl**y**

Top Tip

Some adverbs don't follow the **–ly** pattern. *Example:* good (adjective) – well (adverb). The boy was *good* at reading. He read **well**.

A   Copy each sentence and write the missing adverb in the gap.

1 The ladybird moved _____ along the grass. (careful)
2 The colony of ants worked together _____. (busy)
3 The butterfly landed _____ on the flower. (gentle)

B   Think of an **–ly** adverb to make these sentences more interesting.

1 The wasps buzzed.
2 I walked to the park.
3 The boy sat down.
4 The girl ate an apple.

C   Change the following words into adverbs and write three new sentences.

graceful   noisy   happy

Punctuation

Non-fiction Punctuation

 **A** Match the punctuation mark with the meaning.

. ! ? ,

1 Used to mark a pause in a sentence or to separate a list.
2 Used to mark the end of a sentence.
3 Takes the place of a full stop when the sentence is a question.
4 Used to show a strong feeling.

 **B** Choose the correct punctuation for the end of these sentences.

1 The field was full of fireflies   (. ?)
2 Where were you yesterday   (! ?)
3 Come back   (. !)
4 Who was that   (, ?)

 **C** Put a comma into each of these sentences.

1 As soon as you hear the bell you must come into class.
2 Even though the lesson was over the children wanted to stay.
3 They saw some butterflies spiders and dragonflies.

Non-fiction Spelling

Alphabetical order

 The letters of the alphabet are out of order on these caterpillars. Write the alphabet out in the correct order.

Z E M Q B W D V Y H T J L
I P A F U X N C K G O R S

B Write each group of words in alphabetical order. Remember, you may need to look at the second and third letters too!

1 moth   glow-worm   firefly   night
2 bug   bee   body   breathe
3 ant   abdomen   amber   air
4 spider   spun   scorpion   spin

C Choose a word from one of the extracts and look it up in a dictionary. What does it mean? How quickly did you find it? Work with a partner and take it in turns to time each other.

Non-fiction Writing workshop

Writing a non-chronological report
Model writing

Ants

How many ants are there in the world?
Lots! Ant colonies (groups) can consist of millions of ants, and there are more than 12,000 species!

What happens in an ant colony?
There are three kinds of ants in a colony: the queen, female workers and males. However, only the queen and males have wings – and the queen is the only ant that can lay eggs. You may have guessed that the job of the male ants is to mate with future queen ants but, after mating, the male ants die! Once the queen grows to adulthood, she spends the rest of her life laying eggs. A colony may have one queen or many queens – and many soldier ants. These protect the queen, defend the colony, gather or kill food, and attack enemy colonies in search of food and nesting space. If they defeat another ant colony, they take away their eggs.

Non-fiction Writing workshop

Guided writing

Common features of a non-chronological report

- Not written chronologically (in the order things happen) but in different topic areas.

- Subheadings are often questions, with paragraphs giving the answers.

- Paragraphs usually start with a topic sentence (a general sentence to introduce the subject).
  Example: 'There are three kinds of ants in a colony.'

- Written in the present tense. **Example:** 'These protect the queen…'

- Uses formal rather than informal (chatty) language, but difficult words might be explained. **Example:** 'colonies (groups)'.

- Uses 'you' to make the information more reader-friendly.
  Example: 'You may have guessed…'

- Uses connectives to move from one idea to another.
  Example: 'However'.

Top Tip

You could start your writing by making a **KWWL** grid. This records what you **K**now about a subject, **W**hat you would like to find out, **W**here you will search for the information and what you **L**earned.

Non-fiction Writing workshop

Planning a non-chronological report
Your writing

- Decide which subheadings you are going to have for each paragraph.

  Example:
  What do ants eat?
  What do worker ants do?
  Are there any fantastic facts about ants?

- Next, write in the topic sentence for each paragraph. This is the main sentence that you will go on to develop.

  What do ants eat?

  Ants will eat practically anything. They especially like…

  What do worker ants do?

  Worker ants are very busy. In the nest they…

  Are there any fantastic facts about ants?

  Yes! Ants are amazing creatures. For example…

- Research the questions, writing down some key facts.

- Will you need to explain any difficult words? You could do this by putting an explanation in brackets or including a labelled drawing or diagram.

Non-fiction Writing workshop

Non-chronological report success criteria

Before you write your report, draw a chart of success criteria, like the one below. Write your report and then check it, putting ticks in the boxes. Can you improve your writing?

	Yes	No	Sometimes
Each paragraph has a subheading	✓		
If the subheading is a question, the paragraph answers the question			✓
Each paragraph is developed from a main topic sentence		✓	
Formal language is used	✓		
Difficult words are explained			✓
Written in the present tense	✓		
Punctuation at the end of sentences is correct	✓		
If you want to do very well			
Use the personal pronoun 'you'			
Use adverbs or adverbial phrases			
Use a variety of connectives to join ideas for the reader			

Play scripts Speaking and listening

3 Tricks and truth

"Everything you can imagine is real."
Pablo Picasso

Let's Talk

1 What is the difference between using your imagination and not telling the truth?
2 Watching a play can take us away from real life for a while. Are there other times when it is good to let our imagination run free?

Play scripts Speaking, listening and vocabulary

Words and imagination

A Look at the words in the Word Cloud and match them to the meanings here.

1 Something that looks real, but isn't.
2 To picture something in your mind.
3 To make something seem greater than it is.

Word Cloud
exaggerate
illusion
imagine

B Read the story below. Imagine you are going to talk to Scheherazade. Think of three questions to ask her.

Scheherazade was a Persian queen. She was afraid that the king would not let her live. So, every night, she told him wonderful stories. She would always stop at the most exciting part, so the king would want to hear the rest of the story. That way, she knew her life would be spared!

Scheherazade told the king stories for 1,001 nights. Her stories are still read today. Have you heard of *Ali Baba and the Forty Thieves* and *Aladdin's Wonderful Lamp*?

C Think of a story that you know well and tell it to a partner. Make it as imaginative and exciting as you can.

Play scripts Reading

Play scripts on common themes

The Wonderful Smells

Li Hua is eight and from a poor family. Her brother, Li Chang, is six. Shen Ying is a mean woman who works in the Full Moon Cafe. Pang Bo is a mean man who cooks in the cafe and cheats the customers.

Word Cloud
accusing
customers
expensive

SCENE 6
(The Courtroom…)

Judge	And now, the last case of the day. Is Li Hua in court?… Are Pang Bo and Shen Ying in court?… Good… And you are accusing Li Hua of stealing from your cafe?…
Pang Bo	She took some money, sir, and didn't give it back.
Judge	How much money?
Pang Bo	Five chien.
Judge	…What do you say to that, Li Hua?
Li Hua	It was *my* money, sir. I bought some moon cakes and the money was my change. Pang Bo gave it to me!
Judge	The five chien was your change, you say. Is this true, Pang Bo?
Pang Bo	Well, in a way.
Shen Ying	But it was a mistake! He shouldn't have given it to her.
Judge	Explain yourselves…

Play scripts Reading

Shen Ying	The thing is, this girl has been standing around outside the cafe, smelling all the expensive food.
Pang Bo	Yes, and she hasn't paid us anything. Not a single chien!
Shen Ying	She's been stealing our smells!
Judge	What do you say to that, Li Hua? Is it true that you have been smelling the food from the Full Moon Cafe?
Li Hua	Yes, sir, but I can't help it. I pass by there every day. And anyway, smelling is free, isn't it?…
Judge	Li Hua… Did you like the smell of the food?
Li Hua	Yes, sir.
Judge	And do you still have the five chien?
Li Hua	Yes, sir, but…
Judge	There are no buts about it… I have here a bag.
Shen Ying	It's a money bag!
Judge	Li Hua, I want you to put the five chien into the bag.
Li Hua	But, sir…
Judge	I thought I said no buts. Take the bag, Li Hua… Now, put the money into the bag.
Li Hua	Do I have to?
Judge	Yes.
Li Chang	No! Stop! This isn't fair! …

From *The Wonderful Smells*, by Julia Donaldson

Glossary

chien
Chinese money

courtroom
a room in which a judge hears evidence and decides if someone has committed a crime

judge
a person whose job it is to decide if someone has committed a crime

Play scripts Comprehension

Comprehension

A Read and answer the questions.

1 What did Li Hua buy in the cafe?
2 According to Pang Bo and Shen Ying, what did Li Hua not pay for?
3 What does the judge want to do?

B What do you think?

1 Look again at the playscript. How do we know who is talking?
2 Find an example of some words that are in brackets ( ) and *italics*. Why are these words in brackets and italics?
3 Find an example of a word that is not in brackets but is in *italics*. Why is this?

Play scripts **Comprehension**

C What about you?

If your class was going to act this play, what role (part) would you like to take? Remember there are roles behind the scenes too, for example director, set designer and costume designer.

Discussion time

How do you think this play is going to end? Discuss your ideas as a class.

Challenge

In a small group, read this extract together. One person should take the part of the director and tell the others *how* to say the words.

Play scripts on common themes (continued)

The Wonderful Smells

Judge	Silence in court! Now, is all the money in the bag?… give the bag to me, Li Hua.
(Li Hua gives him the bag.)	
5 **Judge**	Thank you. Now I am going to shake this bag of coins. *(He shakes it.)* Did you hear the coins jingling in the bag, Pang Bo?
Pang Bo	Yes, sir.
10 **Judge**	Did you hear them, Shen Ying?
Shen Ying	Yes, sir. Thank you, sir.
Judge	And did you both like the jingling sound?
Pang Bo	Oh yes, sir…
15 **Judge**	I'm glad to hear that. So, Li Hua liked the smell of your food, and you liked the sound of her coins jingling. Come here, Li Hua. You can have your money back now.
20 *(He gives her the bag.)*	
Pang Bo	But it's *our* money!
Shen Ying	It's our pay for the smells!
Judge	No. Your pay for the smells was the *sound* of the money.
25 **Pang Bo**	But…
Judge	No buts about it! Let the girl go free…

Word Cloud
coins
jingling
shake

From *The Wonderful Smells*, by Julia Donaldson

Play scripts Comprehension

Comprehension

Read and answer the questions.

1 Why does the judge put the money in the bag?
2 Why do Pang Bo and Shen Ying think that the money should be theirs?
3 How does the judge explain their payment?

Discussion time
What would you have done if you had been the judge? Discuss your ideas in small groups.

What do you think?

1 Why do you think the judge asks so many questions?
2 Do you think anyone in the play tried to trick anyone else? If so, who?
3 How do you think these lines from the play should be spoken? Read them aloud.

- She's been stealing our smells!
- No! Stop! This isn't fair!
- But it's *our* money!
- No. Your pay for the smells was the *sound* of the money.

What about you?

Did you like the way the scenes built up in this play script and the way it ended? Give your reasons.

Play scripts Grammar

Irregular verbs

Regular verbs end in –ed in the past tense.

 **Find the verbs in these sentences. Copy out the sentences, changing the verbs into the past tense.**

1 The fox plays tricks on other animals.
2 A crocodile waits in the water.
3 The monkeys watch from the trees.

Irregular verbs do not follow a pattern.

 **Match the present tense with the past tense of these verbs.**

run   hear   saw   said   ran
say   write   see   wrote   heard

 **Copy and complete this children's rhyme. Use the past tense of the irregular verbs in brackets to fill the gaps.**

Did you ever tell a lie?

Yes, you _____, you know you _____, (do)

You _____ your mother's teapot lid. (break)

Well, it _____ only blue. (is)

No, it wasn't, it _____ gold. (is)

That's another lie you've _____! (tell)

Play scripts Grammar and vocabulary

Powerful verbs

We can improve our writing by thinking carefully about the words we use. Try to include **powerful verbs** (more interesting verbs) wherever you can.

A Match the ordinary verb with a powerful verb that has a similar meaning.

shout   walk   hold   fly

clutch   glide   bellow   stroll

B Use a powerful verb from the box to replace the underlined words in this story.

gobbled   noticed   felt   soaring
crept   remarked   landed

One day, a cunning fox <u>went</u> through a forest. He <u>saw</u> a crow <u>flying</u> overhead with some delicious grapes in her beak. She <u>stopped</u> in a nearby tree. The fox <u>said</u>, "Oh, Crow, you sing so beautifully." The crow <u>was</u> pleased and opened her mouth to sing. The grapes fell out and the fox <u>ate</u> them up.

C Look again at the powerful verbs you used in the story above. Which of them are regular verbs and which are irregular verbs?

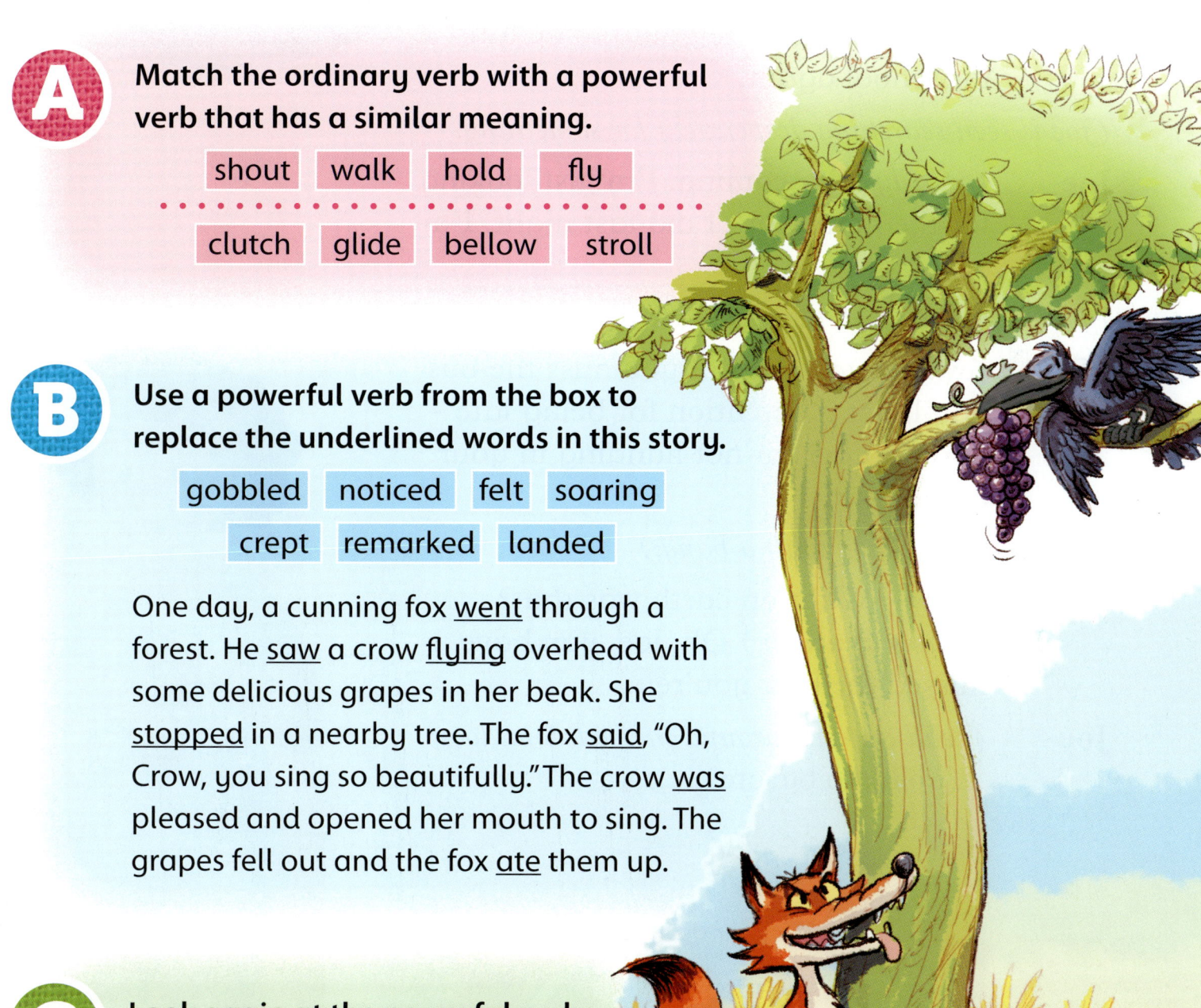

49

Play scripts Writing workshop

Model play script

SCENE 1

(Joe's bedroom is upstage right. Mum enters left, shouting.)

Mum Joe! The school bus will be here any minute! You're going to be late for school again!

(Joe is seen searching desperately for something.)

Joe *(angrily)* I'm coming. I'm just looking for the homework I did last night. I'm sure I put it…

(Joe lifts up his bed, peering underneath.)

Mum *(exasperated)* Well, if you miss the bus you'll get a detention for being late – and another for not handing in your homework!

(The bed falls down with a bang.)

Mum *(jumps)* What on earth was that? *(Looks at watch.)* Oh, Joe, you have missed the bus, you're…

Joe *(head appears around the bedroom door)* … going to be late!

Top Tip

Upstage means towards the back of the stage.
Downstage means towards the front of the stage.

Play scripts Writing workshop

Guided writing

Features of a play script:

- The character's name is written on the left-hand side. This tells the actors whose turn it is to speak.

- What the character says appears after their name. You don't use speech marks.

- The stage directions are shown in brackets. They say where each scene is taking place.

- Stage directions often tell the actors where to move or how to speak or act.

- Adverbs are often used in stage directions. **Example:** desperately, angrily.

Your writing

Carry on writing this play script so Joe arrives at school late – and with no homework. Will he tell the truth or invent an excuse? You will need to think about the following:

- Who will your characters be? Choose no more than four. You could choose from: Joe, Mum, teacher, head teacher, Joe's friend, Joe's sister, Joe's Dad.

- Describe each of your characters in five words/ phrases. You could even draw a picture of them!

- Decide what the main message of your play will be. **Example:** 'Be organized' or 'Always be truthful'.

Top Tip

Make a flow chart to show how the play will develop and then finish.

Revise and check 1

Units 1, 2 and 3

Vocabulary

1 Write these words in alphabetical order.

skeleton   surface   slate   scrumptious   snooty   shake   species

2 Copy out the sentences below and change the red words to a word that means the same from the list above.

   a The **haughty** nurse looked down her nose at the children.

   b The little boy's hand began to **wobble**.

   c The girls ate the **delicious** cakes and ran off to play in the forest.

   d Each child had a small **board** and a piece of chalk.

3 Write three more sentences of your own using the words you have not yet used from the list.

Punctuation

1 Copy out the paragraph below adding commas in the correct places.

On her birthday Skye got up early. Her presents which had arrived the night before were in the kitchen. Her brother and sister who were much older had bought her some dancing shoes.

Units 1, 2 and 3

Grammar

1 Write out the sentences below underlining the main clauses.
   a Children played with boats and trains made of wood.
   b At the weekends, the brothers liked to play outside.
   c In the holidays, when the weather was sunny, families would go to the beach.

2 Add a subordinate clause to each of the sentences below.
   a Bugs can do a great deal of damage.
   b The field was full of insects.
   c Bees can be a nuisance.

3 Copy out the sentences with the correct verb in the **past** tense.

   have   leap   be   see   hear   write

   a A long time ago children _____ on slates.
   b Classes _____ big and schools _____ fewer teachers.
   c Once, we _____ a huge spider in the bathroom.
   d Suddenly an insect _____ out of the pond.
   e We _____ the sound of buzzing bees.

4 Match the questions words in the small yellow cloud with the adverbs and adverbial phrases in the big blue cloud.

   How?
   Where?
   When?

   in a moment
   here
   carefully
   on the table
   in alphabetical order
   tomorrow

Spelling

1 Use the suffix **–ly** to change these adjectives into adverbs.

   beautiful   safe   brave   sleepy   reasonable

   Now write a sentence using each adverb.

Fiction Speaking and listening

4 Fantastic journeys

"Would you tell me, please, which way I ought to go from here?" said Alice. "That depends a good deal on where you want to get to," said the cat.

Alice in Wonderland by Lewis Carroll

Let's Talk

1 The picture shows a fantastic journey. What do you think the destination of the journey is?
2 Why is it important to know exactly where you are going before you set off on a journey?

Fiction Speaking, listening and vocabulary

Fantastic words

Word Cloud
enchanted
expedition
explorer
perils

 **A** **Look at the words in the Word Cloud and match them to the meanings here.**

1 A journey with a destination.
2 Serious dangers or risks.
3 Magical and charming.
4 A person who goes on adventures and makes discoveries.

 **B** **Look at the pictures here and match a sentence to each picture.**

1 Alice falls asleep and finds herself in an extraordinary and enchanted place.
2 She speaks with fantastical characters and incredible things happen.
3 Alice's story is in her imagination, just a dream.

 **C** **Think of some fantastic journeys and talk about them with a partner. What are the dangers of going on a journey to an unfamiliar place? Why is it exciting to explore new places?**

Fiction Reading

Fantasy fiction

A hundred years ago, in the Himalayan peaks of Nanvi Dar, Agatha, the daughter of an English earl is kidnapped by a huge, hairy monster. She wakes up to find herself in an unfamiliar place.

Kidnap

Word Cloud
distinguished
generous-looking
sheer
unmistakable

She looked around. The air was warm, and she saw trees covered in red and white and cream blossoms as big as plates. There was a stream, crystal clear and bubbly, with
5 kingfishers darting about its banks. Far above her an eagle circled lazily. She was in a broad valley, surrounded on every side by sheer, jagged cliffs and escarpments. And then to her surprise… she saw the unmistakable outline of
10 the peak of Nanvi Dar, glittering white in the early morning sun.

"Perhaps I haven't died after all," said Lady Agatha.

And there was something else that didn't
15 go with the idea of heaven in the least. A few metres away from her… was an absolutely enormous dark brown beast… And then she remembered. A yeti. She had been carried away by a yeti over mountains so dangerous
20 that she could never make her way back alone. She was trapped here in this secret valley, perhaps for ever.

Fiction Reading

"I should feel terribly frightened," thought Agatha.

25 But feeling frightened is an odd thing. You either feel it or you don't, and Agatha didn't. Instead she got up and walked quietly towards the yeti. Then she leaned forward and put her hand on the yeti's arm. At once she was buried
30 up to the elbow in long, cool, silky, tickly hair, masses and masses of it… then Lady Agatha Farlingham became the first human ever to see a yeti's face.

She thought it a most interesting and
35 distinguished face. Yetis have huge, round, intelligent eyes as big as saucers… Yetis also have snub noses and big ears and the ears have a most useful flap on them, an ear *lid*, which they can close. This saves them from
40 getting earache in the fierce Himalayan winds… Their mouths are big and generous-looking.

Best of all are their smiles.

From *The Abominables* by Eva Ibbotson

Glossary

escarpment
a very steep slope; the face of a mountain

Nanvi Dar
an imaginary place in the Himalayas

yeti
a fantastical creature said to live in the Himalayas

Comprehension

A Read and answer the questions.

1 How did Agatha get to the valley?
2 What did Agatha think of the yeti?
3 Why was Agatha not frightened of it?
4 Why does the yeti have ear lids?

Discussion time

The imaginary valley in the story is brought to life by the author. Describe an imaginary place that you have heard about in a book or a film. How does the author make the place seem real?

Fiction Comprehension

 **What do you think?**

Use phrases from the story to help with your answers.

1 Why do you think Lady Agatha says, 'Perhaps I haven't died after all?'
2 How do we know that nobody had ever seen a yeti before?
3 What simile does the author use to describe the yeti's eyes?
4 What does the author say about the yeti's mouth and why is this important?

 **What about you?**

Agatha woke up next to a yeti. Have you ever imagined a fantastical beast? What was it like? What made it different from a real creature?

Fantasy fiction (continued)

Kidnap

He got up and stood there, waiting, with his head on one side, till Agatha got up too, and then he began to lead her along the floor of the valley… And as he walked, Agatha saw
5 that his enormous feet – each about the size of a well-fed dachshund – had eight toes and were put on back to front. And this, of course, was why later when people tried to track yetis in the snow they never found them. Yetis who
10 seem to be going are really coming, and yetis who seem to be coming are really going. It is as simple as that.

Suddenly the yeti stopped, bent down to a little hollow by the bank of the
15 stream and began to clear away the dried grass and sticks which covered it. When he had finished he grunted in a pleased sort of way and then he moved aside so that Agatha
20 could see what he had uncovered.

"Oh!" said Agatha. Sleeping peacefully, curled up in each
25 other's arms, were two fat, furry baby yetis.

From *The Abominables* by Eva Ibbotson

Word Cloud
dachshund
hollow
peacefully
valley

Fiction Comprehension

Comprehension

 **A** Which two sentences below are false?

1. The yeti led Agatha up a mountain.
2. Agatha saw that the yeti had eight toes.
3. The yeti stopped by a large tree.
4. The yeti babies were sleeping peacefully.

 **B** What do you think?

Use phrases from the story to help with your answers.

1. How does the author let us know that the yeti was patient?
2. How do we know that the yeti had big feet? Find the phrase in the story that the author uses to describe them.
3. How do you know that Agatha was surprised to find the babies?

Challenge

The author tells us that people could never track down the yetis. Why was this? What would you look for if you were trying to track down a creature in the forest?

 **C** What about you?

The yeti and Agatha have started to become friends. Talk with a partner about the characters and how their friendship makes you feel.

Fiction Grammar and punctuation

The apostrophe – contractions

Apostrophes are used in **contractions**. This is when words are shortened by leaving out a letter. The apostrophe is there to show us that a letter is missing.

Example: **She's** always late. (**She is** always late.)

We usually use contractions when we are speaking.

"**That's** not right! There **isn't** a yeti here!" said the prince.

A Match up these contractions.

who's
you're
they'll
let's

let us
they will
you are
who is

B Rewrite these sentences using contractions.

1 Who is going to arrive first?
2 The explorers did not know the way.
3 The yeti can not be found.

Fiction Grammar and punctuation

The apostrophe – possession

Apostrophes are also used to show us that something belongs to someone. This is called **possession**.

Example: Agatha put her hand on the yeti's arm.

The owner of the arm is the yeti. The apostrophe always comes after the owner word.

Top Tip

Remember if you are making a word plural by adding an **s**, you don't need to use an apostrophe.

A Write these sentences underlining the owner and adding the apostrophe.

1. The childs coat was on the seat.
2. The horses ate the yetis food.
3. She came in her fathers car.

B Rewrite these phrases using an apostrophe + s ('s).

1. The edge of the water.
2. The carrots of the rabbit.
3. The tail of the cat.

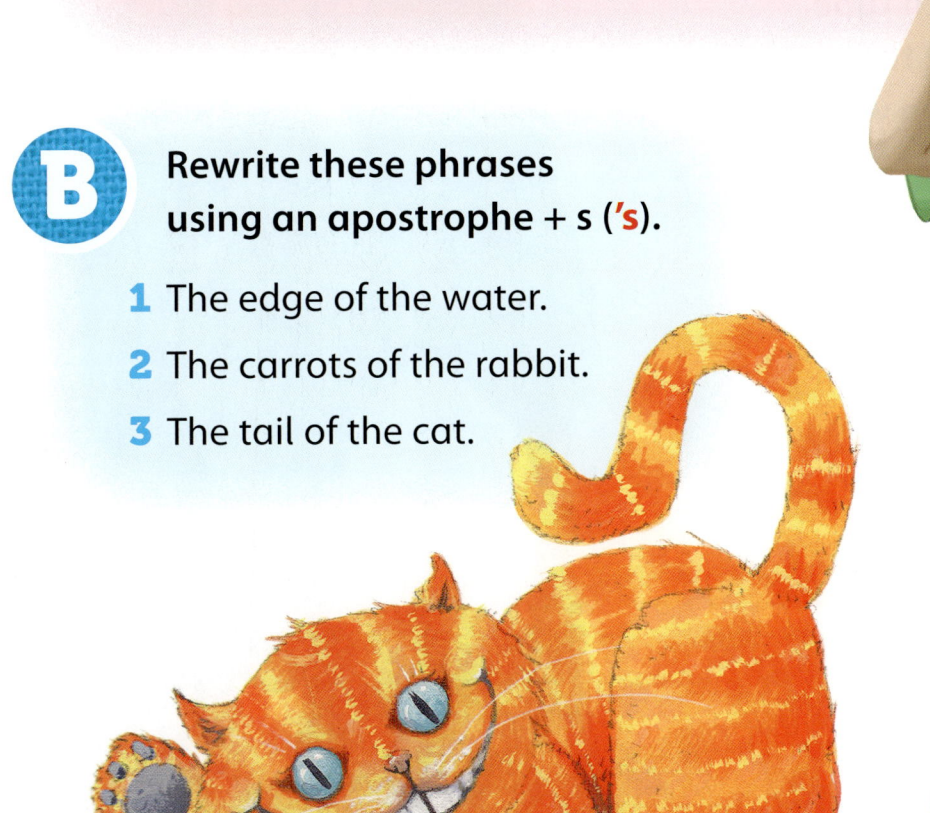

Fiction **Grammar and vocabulary**

Similes

We use similes and metaphors to make our writing more interesting.

A **simile** compares two things, which have something in common. We use the words **as** or **like** to make the comparison.

Look at these sentences:

The children ran **like** the wind.

She climbed **like** a monkey.

He was **as** quiet **as** a mouse.

The girl was **as** good **as** gold.

 Choose two of the similes above, one of each type, and explain what the writer means in your own words.

 Use the same patterns to complete the sentences below:

1 The yeti's feet were **as** _____.

2 The yeti's fur was soft **like** _____.

3 The yeti's eyes were **as** _____.

Fiction Grammar and vocabulary

 This is a simile rainbow! Write similes for the colours on the rainbow and put them into sentences. The first one has been done for you.

As red as a ripe apple.

As orange as a…

As yellow as a…

As green as a…

As blue as a…

As purple as a…

Fiction Writing workshop

Writing a fantasy story
Model writing

Only ten minutes ago 8-year-old Malik had been sitting at home, bored, gazing out at the window at the endless rain gushing down. Then, as a thin ribbon of lightning had flashed across the afternoon sky, he had suddenly shouted out, "I want an adventure!" Well, who could have guessed what happened next?

A thick cloud of smoke, an angry bang and a large whoosh, and now here he was, in the middle of a forest, next to a broken signpost saying, 'Welcome to Alania'. And, to top it all, there was a note pinned underneath saying, 'Help needed!'

Malik had wanted an adventure, but now, as the sky darkened and odd noises filled the air, he wasn't quite so sure…

Fiction Writing workshop

Guided writing

Here are some of the typical features of a fantasy story, which you can use in your own writing:

- A real-life character is placed in a fantasy world.

- There can be strange plants, animals, fantastical beasts and even monsters!

- Some characters are invented (not real) and have made-up names. There are often dragons, elves and goblins. There might also be a prince or princess, or perhaps an older, wiser character.

- There is often a battle between good and evil. Sometimes, the fantasy world is in danger, and the hero or heroine helps to save the day.

- Doors, rings, and secret messages can play an important part in the story.

Fiction Writing workshop

Your writing

Write your own beginning to a fantasy story. Start by making a plan like the one below. Don't forget to stop your story at an exciting point so that the reader has to guess what happens next!

1. List some 'fantasy' features you are going to include.

   Examples: a deserted castle, a five-headed monster, a talking plant.

2. List the three main characters in your story and write some information about them.

   Examples: a lonely princess, a scary beast with one eye, a green goblin.

3. Write some of the actual words the characters are going to say.

   Example: "Please help, a monster is chasing me!"

4. Decide how many paragraphs you are going to have, and write one sentence to sum up what is going to happen in each paragraph.

   Example: The princess runs through the forest and arrives at an old deserted castle.

Top Tip

You can start a story in lots of different ways. You could use an expression of time: **One fine day**… Or start with some action: **Bella ran as she had never run before**…

Fiction Writing workshop

Fantasy fiction success criteria

Create a chart like the one below to help you write the next part of your fantasy story. Get another student to 'mark' your work first using the success criteria. You could then edit your work and make some improvements.

	Yes	No	Sometimes
Some fantasy features	✓		
Includes at least three characters	✓		
Paragraphs build up in tension / excitement			✓
Story stops at an exciting and tense point	✓		
Apostrophes for contractions used correctly	✓		
Apostrophes for possession used correctly	✓		
Verbs in the right tense	✓		
Some connectives used, such as *because, as, if, so, then, although*	✓		
Full stops and capital letters used properly	✓		
Spelling correct	✓		

5 Amazing animals

Non-fiction Speaking and listening

"I love painting with a palette full of words."
Michael J. Budnicki

SAVE US

Let's Talk

1 Look at the poster above. Do you think it is effective? Explain why.
2 Why do you think the artist chose these pictures and used only two words?

Non-fiction Speaking, listening and vocabulary

What's the story?

 **A** Look at the words in the Word Cloud and match them to the meanings here.

1 An account of something that has happened.
2 A piece of writing that appears regularly in a newspaper or magazine.
3 The title of a newspaper article.

Word Cloud
column
headline
report

B Match the headlines with the first lines of these news stories.

THE NEWS **BABY BOOM!**

THE NEWS **WHO'S THE FASTEST JAW ON THE DRAW?**

THE NEWS **SEA TURTLE SOUP? NO THANKS!**

Which animal has the fastest snapping jaw?

Sea turtles have been on Earth for millions of years, but they are in danger of going extinct.

Su Lin the giant panda… is one of 19 captive pandas to turn a year old…

 **C** With a partner, choose one of the news stories above. How might it develop?

Non-fiction Reading

Newspaper-style reports

THE SECRET LANGUAGE OF DOLPHINS

Here's a conversation worth talking about: A mother dolphin chats with her baby… over the telephone! The special call was made in an aquarium in Hawaii, where
5 the mother and her two-year-old calf swam in separate tanks connected by a special underwater audio link. The two dolphins began squawking and chirping to each other – distinctive dolphin chatter.

Word Cloud
accomplish
captive
distinctive
mammals

10 **Cracking the Code**
"It seemed clear that they knew who they were talking with," says Don White, whose Project
15 Delphis ran the experiment. "Information was passing back and forth pretty quickly." But what were they saying? That's what
20 scientists are trying to find out by studying wild and captive dolphins all over the world to decipher their secret language. They
25 haven't completely cracked the code yet, but they're listening…and learning.

Non-fiction Reading

Chatty Mammals

In many ways, you are just like the more than 30 species of dolphins that swim in the world's oceans and rivers. Dolphins are mammals, like you are, and must swim to the surface to breathe air. Just as you might, they team up in pods, or groups, to accomplish tasks. And they're smart.

They also talk to each other. Starting from birth, dolphins squawk, whistle, click, and squeak. "Sometimes one dolphin will vocalize and then another will seem to answer," says Sara Waller, who studies bottlenose dolphins off the California coast. "And sometimes members of a pod vocalize in different patterns at the same time, much like many people chattering at a party."

From www.kids.nationalgeographic.com

Glossary

audio link
a way to transfer sound between two places

decipher
understand something that is written in code

vocalize
make a sound

Non-fiction Comprehension

Comprehension

A Read and answer the questions.

1 Find a sentence in the newspaper report that tells us the dolphins were talking to each other.
2 How many species of dolphins are there?
3 Find the parts of the report that tell us how dolphins are like humans.

B What do you think?

1 Explain why the report has the headline 'The Secret Language of Dolphins'.
2 Do you think this story belongs on the front page of a newspaper? If not, where?
3 The newspaper report uses both formal and informal (chatty) language. Why do you think it uses these different styles?

Non-fiction Comprehension

C What about you?

The scientists studied both 'wild and captive dolphins'. How do you feel about animals being kept captive – for example, in zoos?

Challenge
The newspaper reports in this Unit come from *National Geographic Kids*, a magazine about science and history. Think of three subjects you could make magazines about.

Discussion time
Some people think wild animals belong in the wild. Other people think that we need to keep some animals captive to learn more about them. Have a class discussion on this topic.

Newspaper-style reports (continued)

TIGERS CUDDLE WITH APES

Tigers don't normally snuggle with orangutans. The big cats are meat-eaters, after all. But when Demis and Manis the tiger cubs were rejected by their mother, zookeepers
5 at Taman Safari Zoo* thought they might like the company of two other orphan siblings: Nia and Irma the orangutans.

"The first time I put them together, they just played," says zookeeper Sri Suwarni. The four
10 shared toys, wrestled, and took naps together. Then one morning, Nia and Irma began hugging Demis the tiger, and he lick-kissed them back! "That's when I knew they were true friends," Suwarni says.

15 As the tigers grew, their natural instincts started showing, so Suwarni moved them into a separate exhibit.

Text by Aline Alexander Newman.
From www.kids.nationalgeographic.com
*Taman Safari Zoo is in Indonesia.

Word Cloud
instincts
rejected
siblings
snuggle

Non-fiction Comprehension

Comprehension

A **Which two sentences below are true?**

1 Tigers are meat-eaters.
2 The tiger cubs were not playful when they first met the orangutans.
3 The tigers did not stay with the orangutans forever.

Challenge
Imagine you are designing a new magazine. What headline would you put on the front of the first issue that would persuade people to buy it?

B **What do you think?**

Use phrases from the newspaper report to help with your answers.

1 Why did the zookeepers put the tigers with the orangutans?
2 How do we know the tiger cubs and the orangutans were friends?
3 Why was this behaviour unusual?
4 Newspapers often contain both **fact** and **opinion**. Which parts of the newspaper report are fact and which are opinion?

C **What about you?**

Why do you think newspapers often mix fact and opinion?

Non-fiction Grammar and punctuation

Apostrophes – plurals and possession

Remember: We usually show **possession** by adding an apostrophe plus **s**.

Example: The kitten**'s** tail.

Plurals do not need an apostrophe unless we are showing possession.

Example: We have two kitten**s**. The kitten**s'** tails are long. (The tails belong to the kittens so this needs an apostrophe.)

Top Tip

Notice that for a plural that ends in **s**, we do not add another **s** after the apostrophe. The kitten**s'** fur **not** The kittens's fur.

A Which two sentences have the correct punctuation?

1. The dog's tail was wagging.
2. The lions's manes were large.
3. The parrots' beaks were sharp.
4. The giraffes necks were long.

B Explain the difference between these two phrases to a partner.

1. The kangaroo's pouch.
2. The kangaroos' pouches.

C We also use apostrophes to show **contractions**. Find three examples from the newspaper reports on pages 72, 73 and 76.

Non-fiction Grammar and vocabulary

Metaphors

A **simile** uses **as** or **like** to compare two things.
A **metaphor** describes something as if it actually *is* something else.

Example: Life is a rollercoaster!

A Complete these metaphors using the words in the boxes.

sunshine   showered   froze   mountain

1 He is a _____ of strength.
2 I _____ with fear.
3 You are the _____ of my life.
4 My friends _____ me with gifts.

B Think of three metaphors that you use in your own language. Share them with a partner in English.

C What do you think the metaphor 'Life is a rollercoaster' means?

Non-fiction Grammar and vocabulary

Adjectives – comparative and superlative

When we compare nouns, we often use **comparative** and **superlative** adjectives.

big

bigger

biggest

We add **–er** or **more** to make the **comparative** and **–est** or **most** to make the **superlative**.

Top Tip

Be careful! Although we usually add **–er** and **–est**, the spelling sometimes changes a bit. *Example:* noisy   noisier   noisiest

 **A** Sort these words and phrases into adjectives, comparatives and superlatives.

red   sleepiest   more beautiful
laziest   quicker   old

 **B** Which words are missing?

Adjective	Comparative	Superlative
large	larger	
busy		busiest
	shallower	shallowest
comfortable	more comfortable	
	gentler	

 **C** Write a sentence for each of the missing words above.

Non-fiction Grammar and vocabulary

Adjectives – intensity

Using adjectives that show different amounts of intensity (strength) can make our writing more accurate and interesting. Adding the suffix **–ish** to an adjective makes it less intense.

Example: She had a **smallish** cake.   She cut a **big** slice.   She ate a **huge** bite.

Look at these sentences. Think of a more intense adjective to fill in the spaces.

1. The monkey was big.
   The monkey was _____.
2. The boy felt sad.
   The boy felt _____.
3. The mouse was frightened.
   The mouse was _____.

Put these adjectives in order of intesity, starting with the coldest.

scorching   warmish   chilly
cold   freezing   hot

Think of some more adjectives that describe temperature. Where will they fit in your list? Can you include some similes?

81

Non-fiction Writing workshop

Writing a newspaper-style report
Model writing

Moko the Dolphin Saves the Day!

Moko, the bottlenose dolphin, who is a regular visitor around the seas of North Coast Island, New Zealand, surprised everyone yesterday by rescuing two whales that became stuck on the beach.

Local people tried to push the whales back into the sea at Mahia Beach, but were unsuccessful.

"We wondered whether it would be better to kill the two whales than leave them to a miserable death." said Mike Smith, a local conservation officer.

It was just at this moment that Moko the dolphin swam towards the two whales and led them through a narrow channel towards the safety of the sea.

"Moko just came flying through the water, and pushed in between us and the whales," said Juanita Symes, one of the rescuers. "She obviously heard them calling, and led them towards the deep water. It was amazing."

The whales have not been seen since, but Moko continues to visit the beach regularly – much to the delight of visitors!

Guided writing
Common features of a newspaper report

A CATCHY HEADLINE that makes the reader want to read the report!

The first paragraph sums the story up.

Presented in paragraphs.

May include both fact and opinion.

Quotations from people involved give more information.

May have a chatty or a more formal style.

The story always finishes with some reference to what happens afterwards.

Non-fiction Writing workshop

Your writing

Choose one of the following stories about brave animals – and then write a newspaper report about it!

1. A cat helps a family to escape from a house fire.
2. A dolphin saves a drowning child.
3. A dog rescues a group of climbers from a snowy mountain.

You will need to include:

- An eye-catching headline that tells the reader what the story is about.
- A summary of the story in the first paragraph.
- Quotations from at least two people.
- A reference in the last paragraph to what happens afterwards. The reader should feel that any problems have been solved!

Top Tip

Remember: A headline might often be a **pun** ('Lost and Hound') or use **alliteration** ('Cool Cat!'). Headlines are not written in full sentences.

Non-fiction Writing workshop

Newspaper report success criteria

Create a chart like the one below to help you write your newspaper report. When you have written it, ask another student to 'mark' it using the success criteria. You could then edit your report to make it even better!

	Yes	No	Sometimes
A catchy headline	✓		
Report divided into paragraphs	✓		
The first paragraph sums up the story		✓	
At least two lots of quotations	✓		
Quotation marks put around speech	✓		
Last paragraph is about what happens afterwards		✓	
Capital letters used at the beginning of sentences and for names and places			✓
Full stops or exclamation marks used at the end of sentences			
Spelling correct			

Poetry Speaking and listening

Families of the world

"Each generation… stands on the shoulders of those who came before."
Maya Angelou

Let's Talk

1 Where do you think the people in the photographs came from or live? Imagine their lives.

2 Think about your own grandparents and family. Were they born somewhere different to you?

Poetry Speaking, listening and vocabulary

Exploring different cultures

A **Look at the words in the Word Cloud and match them to the meanings here.**

1 The language, customs, food, art and music of a group of people.
2 A member of your family who lived many years ago.
3 A person's family or cultural background.

Word Cloud

ancestor
culture
roots

B **Work with a partner and write the questions to go with these answers.**

1 Janet Wong is a children's author and a poet.
2 Janet's family are from South Korea and China, but she herself was born in the United States.
3 She called her Chinese grandpa 'Gong-gong' and her grandma 'Popo'.

C Imagine you are interviewing a person from one of the photographs. Do you think their life is different to yours? What questions might you ask?

Poetry Reading

Poems from different times and cultures

Janet Wong is a children's author and a poet. She was born in the United States, but her family are from South Korea and China. She grew up in a modern city, but her family had ancient traditions.

Janet Wong describes how she was given 'good luck gold' when she was one month old.

🎵 Good Luck Gold

When I was a baby
one month old,
my grandparents gave me
good luck gold:
5   a golden ring
so soft it bends,
a golden necklace
hooked at the ends,
a golden bracelet
10 with coins that say
I will be rich
and happy someday.

I wish that gold
would work
15 real soon.
I need my luck
this afternoon.

Janet S. Wong

Word Cloud
ancient
announces
hooked
signal
scold
traditions

Poetry Reading

When she was older, Janet Wong took part in another important family tradition, serving tea to her grandfather.

Tea Ceremony

"This tea costs sixty dollars a pound,"
Grandfather announces, and grunts
as I begin to pour.
This is a signal
5   for Mother
to look at my free hand,
a glance that lasts
long enough to scold:
Two hands!

10 Like a puppet
I lift my left hand,
answering her silent command
to hold the lid down,
while my right hand
15 tips the teapot
toward Grandfather
in a slow, deep bow.

Two hands!
I feel all eyes watching
20 as I cradle
the old heat-cracked cup
in soft hands of respect,
holding it out to Grandfather
like an offering
25 to the gods.

Janet S. Wong

Glossary

command
an order or an instruction

offering
something that is offered or given as a gift

respect
admire and look up to someone

scold
blame crossly, or tell someone off

Poetry Comprehension

Comprehension

 Find the two sentences below which describe 'Good Luck Gold'. Then find the two sentences that describe 'Tea Ceremony'.

1. The poet talks about a ceremony from a different culture.
2. The poem describes an important family tradition that is said to bring luck.
3. The poem describes the giving of gifts.
4. The poet has respect for her family members.

Discussion time

How many different nationalities are represented in your class? Talk about a custom or traditions you know about.

Poetry Comprehension

What do you think?

1. Look at the rhyming words in 'Good Luck Gold'. Which of the lines rhyme? Can you find a pattern?
2. In 'Tea Ceremony', how do we know that the tea tradition was important to Janet's grandfather?
3. Which of the two poems did you like best? Find the words or phrases that helped you decide.
4. How does this poem make you feel? Find three examples of words the author uses in the poem to create feeling.

What about you?

Poems can sometimes paint pictures in our minds. Read your favourite of the two poems to yourself again. What pictures does it make you think of?

Poems from different times and cultures (continued)

Margaret Walker was an African-American poet. Her family came from Africa to America a long time ago, so she was brought up with two cultures.

Lineage

My grandmothers were strong.
They followed plows and bent to toil.
They moved through fields sowing seed.
They touched earth and grain grew.
5 They were full of sturdiness and singing.
My grandmothers were strong.

My grandmothers are full of memories
Smelling of soap and onions and wet clay
With veins rolling roughly over quick hands
10 They have many clean words to say.
My grandmothers were strong.
Why am I not as they?

Margaret Walker

Word Cloud
lineage
plows (ploughs)
sturdiness
toil

Poetry Comprehension

 **A** Which two sentences are true?

1 The grandmothers worked hard in the fields.
2 The grandmothers were sturdy and strong.
3 The grandmothers worked in silence.

Challenge
The poet uses **alliteration** in the poem to make her writing more interesting. Find three examples of alliteration in the poem and read the lines aloud to yourself.

 **B** What do you think?

Look at how the poet uses language.

1 What words tell us that the grandmothers' hands were old?
2 Which line tells us that that the grandmothers were successful with their planting?
3 Do you think the grandmothers were happy or unhappy? Give reasons for your answer.

 **C** What about you?

The grandmothers in the poem were 'full of memories'. Do you think this tells us that they are from a different generation? Talk with a partner about memories you have of time with your own family.

Poetry Grammar and vocabulary

Figurative language

Poets often use **figurative language** in their poems. Figurative language compares two things in a way that is interesting or even a bit surprising.

Similes and **metaphors** are two sorts of figurative language.

Remember: A **simile** compares two things which have something in common.

Example: Mum is always as busy as a bee.

A **metaphor** describes something as if it *is* something else.

Example: Mum is a busy bee.

A Which of these sentences are similes and which are metaphors?

1 Jamila can swim like a fish.
2 Ravi is a scaredy cat.
3 Erik's eyes are as blue as the sky.
4 My best friend is a star.

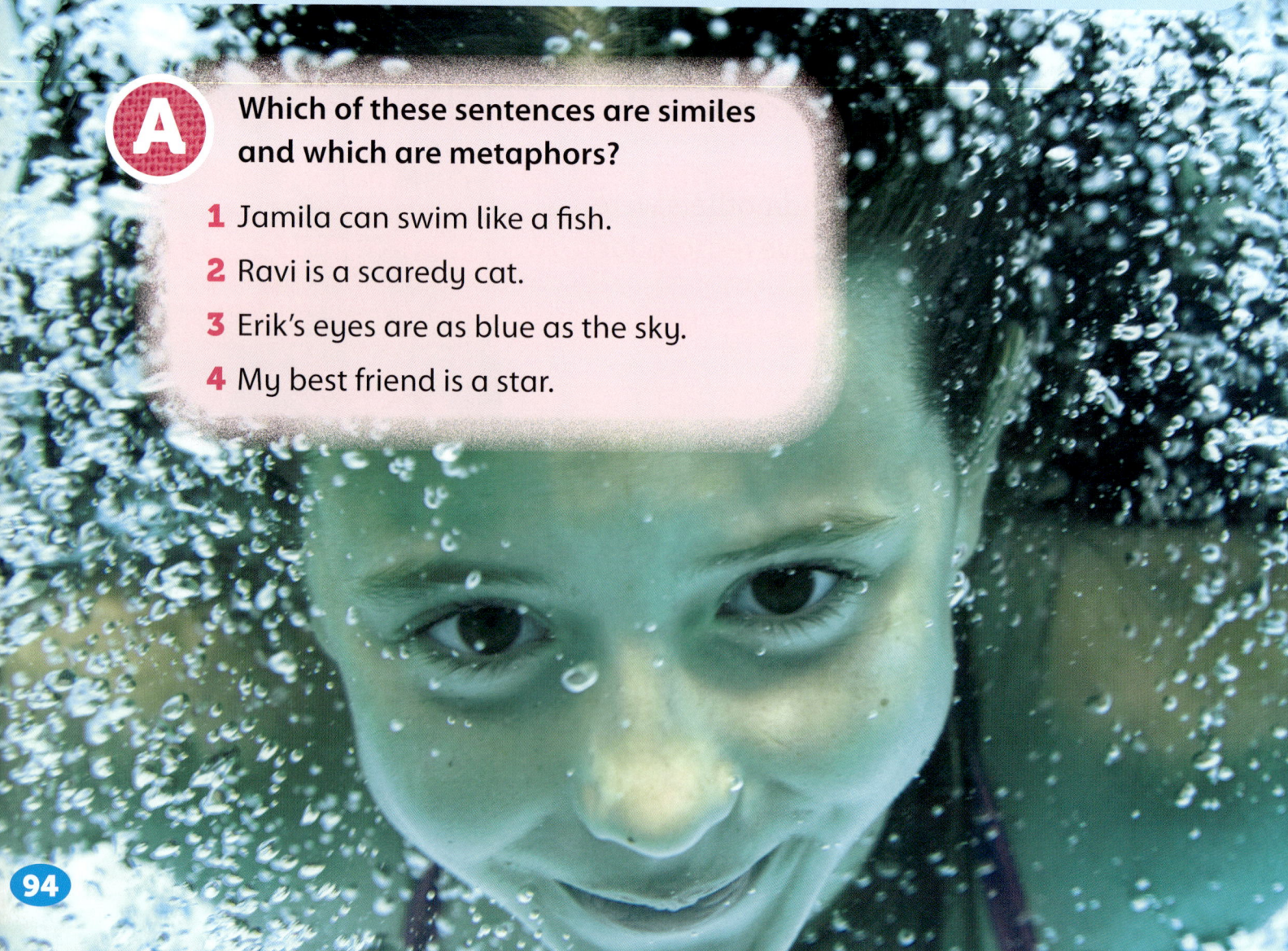

Poetry Grammar and vocabulary

 **Fill in the spaces in the sentences using the words below.**

| fast | flew | slow | light | snail |
| blocks of ice | feather | lightning |

1 You are as _____ as a _____.
2 Your feet are like _____.
3 You walk as _____ as a _____.
4 You ran as _____ as _____.
5 He _____ down the street.

Challenge

Work with a partner and choose four famous people. Write funny metaphors to describe your celebrities. Pick your favourite metaphor and share it with the rest of the class.

 **Look at the metaphors below. Explain what they mean in your own words.**

1 Her grandfather is a gentle giant.
2 A blanket of snow covered the land.
3 Her brother spilled the beans.
4 The spelling test was a dream.

Poetry Writing workshop

Model poem

This poem is about someone's family tree.
The poet uses lots of techniques in her writing.

My Family Tree

Look, look at my family tree
My family are such an important part of me!

My grandmother
Her smell is of old, fragrant flowers
Her eyes are as sharp as stones
She tells me, "Work hard to succeed."

Kind but razor sharp
My grandmother.

Look, look at my family tree
They are all an important part of me!

My grandfather
His smell is of new tobacco
His hands are like old gloves
He tells me, "Be honest, my son."

Gentle but wise
My grandfather.

Poetry Writing workshop

Guided writing

The poet uses techniques including:

1 A chorus, in which lines are repeated.

Example: Look, look at my family tree.

2 A simile, which compares one thing to another.

Example: Her eyes are as sharp as stones

3 A line that includes a quotation.

Example: She tells me, "Work hard to succeed."

4 A line with two contrasting features.

Example: Kind but razor sharp

Writing your own poem

A good way to start writing poetry is to 'copy' another poem. Use the *My Family Tree* poem as a model to write about someone in your family. Change the words so that they suit this person. Remember to copy the same structure and techniques used by the original poet.

Top Tip

When you have written a poem always read it out aloud. Listening to the poem will help you hear how the words and phrases work. It will help you to identify which parts of your poem can be improved.

Units 4, 5 and 6

Revise and check 2

Vocabulary

1 Choose the correct words from the choices below to complete the sentences.

Maya's ancestor was **(an explorer / a mammal)**. He understood the **(roots / perils)** of some of his expeditions. His favourite expedition was to the lost **(valley / tradition)**. He had **(hooked / accomplished)** a great deal in his life. Sometimes, he even made the **(headlines / columns)** in **(unmistakable / distinguished)** newspapers. At the end of his life he lived **(incredibly / peacefully)** in the **(ancient / captive)** city of Rome.

Punctuation

1 Copy out this paragraph adding the apostrophes where they are needed.

There isnt a zoo near us but weve got a park with animals. The keepers my friends uncle and sometimes he lets us help him. I dont like the iguanas much, but I love the baby kangaroos. The kangaroos enclosure is massive! Theres a pets corner for the younger children. My cousins coming to spend the holidays with us, so well go there every day.

Units 4, 5 and 6

Grammar

1 Divide the phrases in the cloud into similes and metaphors. Make a list like the one here.

Metaphors	Similes
A glowing report	As big as a bus

A dark secret
As white as snow
As cold as ice
Colourful remarks
As busy as a bee
Scaredy cat!
A glowing report
As big as a bus

2 Choose one simile and one metaphor from the cloud and write a sentence to show their meaning.

3 Read the paragraph below and complete the sentences with the correct form of the adjective.

African elephants are probably the **(interesting)** animals on the planet, and certainly the **(big)**! The **(heavy)** elephant weighed 24,000 pounds!

The **(good)** place to see them is Amboseli in Kenya. They have **(large)** ears than Indian elephants but **(small)** heads and **(few)** toenails. Elephants are intelligent but can also be **(dangerous)** than other wild animals.

Spelling

1 Write the comparative form of these adjectives:

gentle   noisy   red   late   tidy

2 Write the superlative form of these adjectives:

early   bad   dirty   loud   sad

7 All together!

Fiction Speaking and listening

"Don't walk in front of me; I may not follow. Don't walk behind me; I may not lead. Just walk beside me and be my friend."
Albert Camus

Let's Talk

1 This picture shows a sister and a brother. In what ways do brothers and sisters help each other?

2 Think of a time that you helped a friend with a problem, or they helped you. How did you work together to solve the problem?

Fiction Speaking, listening and vocabulary

Thinking about friends

 **Look at the words in the Word Cloud and match them to the meanings here.**

1 Being friends with someone.
2 A rule that keeps people of different races separate.
3 Got rid of something so that it does not happen or exist anymore.

Word Cloud
abolished
apartheid
friendship

 **Read the extract below. Which are the correct words to fill in the gaps?**

laws   attended   mixing   apartheid

Sbongile is ten years old. She lives in Cape Town, South Africa… Just a few years ago, Sbongile could not have _____ Ellerton Primary School in South Africa. At that time, the _____ laws prevented black and white people from _____. Those _____ have now been completely abolished.

From DK Reference *A Life Like Mine: How children live around the world*

 Where do your friends come from? What can you learn from having friends from different places and backgrounds?

101

Fiction Reading

Stories about problems and issues

Mona lives in America. Her grandmother lives far away from her in a small village in the Middle East. Once, Mona went to visit her. They didn't speak the same language, so they made up their own.

Word Cloud
admired
peeking
spun
whooshed

Sitti's Secrets

My Grandmother lives on the other side of the earth. When I have daylight, she has night. When our sky grows dark, the sun is peeking through her window and brushing the
5 bright lemons on her lemon tree. I think about this when I am going to sleep.

"Your turn!" I say…

Once I went to visit my grandmother. My grandmother and I do not speak the same
10 language. We talked through my father, as if he were a telephone, because he spoke both our languages and could translate what we said.

I called her *Sitti*, which
15 means Grandma in Arabic. She called me *habibi*, which means darling. Her voice danced as high as the
20 whistles of birds. Her voice giggled and whooshed like wind going around corners. She had a thousand
25 rivers in her voice.

A few curls of dark hair peeked out of her scarf on one side, and a white curl peeked out on the other side. I wanted her to take off the scarf so I could see if her hair was striped.

30 Soon we had invented our own language together. Sitti pointed at my stomach to ask if I was hungry. I pointed to the door to ask if she wanted to go outside. We walked to the fields to watch men picking lentils. We admired the sky
35 with hums and claps…

Every day I played with my cousins, Fowzi, Sami, Hani, and Hendia from next door. We played marbles together in their courtyard. Their marbles were blue and green and spun
40 through the dust like planets. We didn't need words to play marbles…

In the evenings we climbed the stairs to the roof of Sitti's house to look at the sky, smell the air, and take down the laundry. My
45 grandmother likes to unpin the laundry in the evening so she can watch the women of the village walking back from the spring with jugs of water on their heads. She used to do that, too. My father says the women don't really
50 need to get water from the spring anymore, but they like to. It is something from the old days they don't want to forget.

From *Sitti's Secrets*, by Naomi Shihab Nye

Fiction Reading

Glossary

courtyard
an open space surrounded by walls or buildings

marbles
a game played with small glass balls

spring
a place where water comes up from the ground

translate
say in another language

Comprehension

A Which sentence below is true?

1 Mona and her grandmother live in the same country.
2 Mona doesn't spend time with her grandmother when she visits her.
3 'Sitti' means 'Grandma'.
4 Mona's grandmother likes to unpin her laundry in the morning.

Fiction Comprehension

Challenge
Try to communicate with a partner without using words. Did your partner understand what you wanted to say?

What do you think?

1 What time of day is it for Mona when her grandmother wakes up?
2 What similes are used to describe Sitti's voice?
3 How do Mona and Sitti communicate with each other? Find examples from the story to support your answer.
4 What does the game of marbles show Mona?

Discussion time
Have you ever been in a similar situation to Mona? If you didn't speak the same language as someone else, do you think this would stop you being friends?

What about you?

Do you like the writer's use of language? Explain your answer and choose three phrases you found particularly effective or interesting.

Stories about problems and issues (continued)

Sitti's Secrets

On the day my father and I had to leave, everyone cried and cried. Even my father kept blowing his nose and walking outside. I cried hard when Sitti held my head against her
5 shoulder. My cousins gave me a sack of almonds to eat on the plane. Sitti gave me a small purse she had made. She had stitched a picture of her lemon tree onto the purse with shiny thread. She popped the almonds into
10 my purse and pulled the drawstrings tight…

Sometimes I think the world is a huge body tumbling in space, all
15 curled up like a child sleeping. People are far apart, but connected.

My grandmother lives on the other side of the earth. While I am dreaming, she
20 rises from her fluffy bed and steps out her door to check the lemons growing on her tree. The first thing she does every day is say good morning to her lemons.

All day the leafy shadow of her tree
25 will grow and change on her courtyard wall. She will move with its shade. When she sleeps, she will dream of me.

From *Sitti's Secrets*, by Naomi Shihab Nye

Word Cloud
drawstrings
leafy
stitched
tumbling

Comprehension

Fiction Comprehension

 **A** Read and answer the questions.

1 What gifts did Mona receive?
2 What will the picture on the purse remind Mona of?
3 What is Sitti doing when Mona is sleeping?
4 What does Mona think Sitti dreams about?

Challenge
Imagine that a relative or friend comes to visit you and you do not speak the same language. What would you show them in your town or village? How would you show them?

 **B** What do you think?

1 How do we know that Mona's father is upset?
2 Did you like the characters in this story? Explain your answer.
3 How does Mona describe the world?
4 Mona says: 'People are far apart, but connected.' What do you think she means by this?

 **C** What about you?

How does the story make you feel? Share your feelings with a partner.

Fiction Phonics and spelling

Homophones

Homophones are words that are pronounced in the same way, but have different meanings and often different spellings.

Example: The mother and **son** watched the **sun** go down. They could **see** the **sea**.

A Match the pairs of homophones.

stair

weak

flour

pair

hare

pear

flower

hair

stare

week

Fiction Phonics and spelling

Choose the correct word to complete the sentence.

1 Who _____ when the bus is coming? (nose/knows)
2 The wind _____ all morning. (blew/blue)
3 There was a _____ in the ground. (hole/whole)
4 She arrived an _____ late. (our/hour)

Find the mistake in each sentence. Copy out the sentences, using the correct words.

1 The boy asked for a peace of cake.
2 There were two many cars on the road.
3 The plain arrived on time.
4 My grandparents are very deer to me.

Top Tip

Keep a list of homophone pairs in your notebook. You can also draw pictures to help you remember what they mean.

109

Fiction Grammar and punctuation

Different sentences

A statement gives information, and usually ends with a full stop.

A question asks something and ends with a question mark?

An exclamation shares a strong feeling and ends with an exclamation mark!

A command gives an order and usually ends with an exclamation mark!

A Copy the story and underline the different types of sentences. Use a different colour for each sentence type.

Ali and Tim were fishing by the lake.

"Don't make a noise!" whispered Ali.

"Why?" asked Tim, "Have you caught something?"

"Yes, and it's huge. Oh no! It's a monster!"

Fiction Grammar and punctuation

 **Change these sentences into questions. Use words from the box to help you.**

where   when   what   how

1 There are about 3,000 different species of snakes.
2 Rattlesnakes live in swamps and forests in America.
3 The students have been learning about rattlesnakes.
4 Snakes usually sleep in the sun in the day.

 **What kind of sentences are these? Rewrite them as a different type of sentence.**

1 Wait behind that tree!
2 Can you hear that noise?
3 I'm scared!
4 It's only an owl hooting.

Challenge
Write a paragraph about working together to solve a problem. Use all four sentence types.

Fiction Writing workshop

Writing a story with an everyday setting
Model writing

Making a Friend

"Good morning, students. Please let me introduce you to our new student." And with that, our head teacher shut the door crisply behind her, leaving us all to look at Jorge Panderez.

He was tall, much taller than anyone else in the class – with a huge mop of black, bushy hair that sat on top of his head like a large, extravagant hat.

"Hi, everyone," he announced, before marching briskly to the empty seat beside me. Noisily, he thumped down on the chair, shuffled his scruffy trainers; then turned to give me a wide smile that exposed his two missing front teeth. At that precise moment, I knew Jorge Panderez and I were going to be best friends.

Fiction Writing workshop

Guided writing

A good character description will:

- Describe what a character looks like, how they move and speak, and how they relate to other characters.

Character features	Examples from the extract
Description of physical features	Huge mop of black, bushy hair; scruffy trainers; wide smile with two missing teeth
How they move	Marching briskly; thumped down
How they speak	He announced
Relationship with other characters	Says "Hi, everyone," to the class; smiles at the narrator of the story; the narrator sees him as a best friend

- Often use similes. **Example:** 'black, bushy hair that sat on top of his head like a large, extravagant hat.'
- Emphasize a physical feature, by repeating it in different ways. **Example:** Jorge's size – 'tall', 'taller', 'huge', 'large'.

Fiction Writing workshop

Planning a story with an everyday setting
Your writing

Do you have a best friend? Were you best friends from the start or did you become friends over time?

Write about the time you first met a good friend. Describe:

- When and where you first saw them.
- What they looked like.
- What they said.
- How they moved.
- How they behaved towards you and others.

Remember to:

- Focus only on three or four key physical features, such as size or height, hair and the look on their face.

- Mention one or two items of clothing they were wearing, but choose your words carefully. What is the difference between 'She wore a grey jumper.' and 'An old grey jumper was carelessly slung over her shoulders.'?

Top Tip

You might want to go on to describe a time when your friend proved to be a really good friend.

Fiction Writing workshop

Story success criteria

Before you write your text, draw a chart of success criteria, like the one below. These will help you to write a successful character description. You could perhaps read your description to your best friend, and ask them for feedback!

	Yes	No	Sometimes
Have you described:			
When you first met your friend?	✓		
What they looked like?	✓		
What they said and how they spoke?	✓		
How they moved?		✓	
An incident where they proved to be a good friend and helped you?	✓		
Have you remembered to:			
Use at least one simile?			
Use adjectives?			
Check all sentences begin with a capital letter and full stop?			

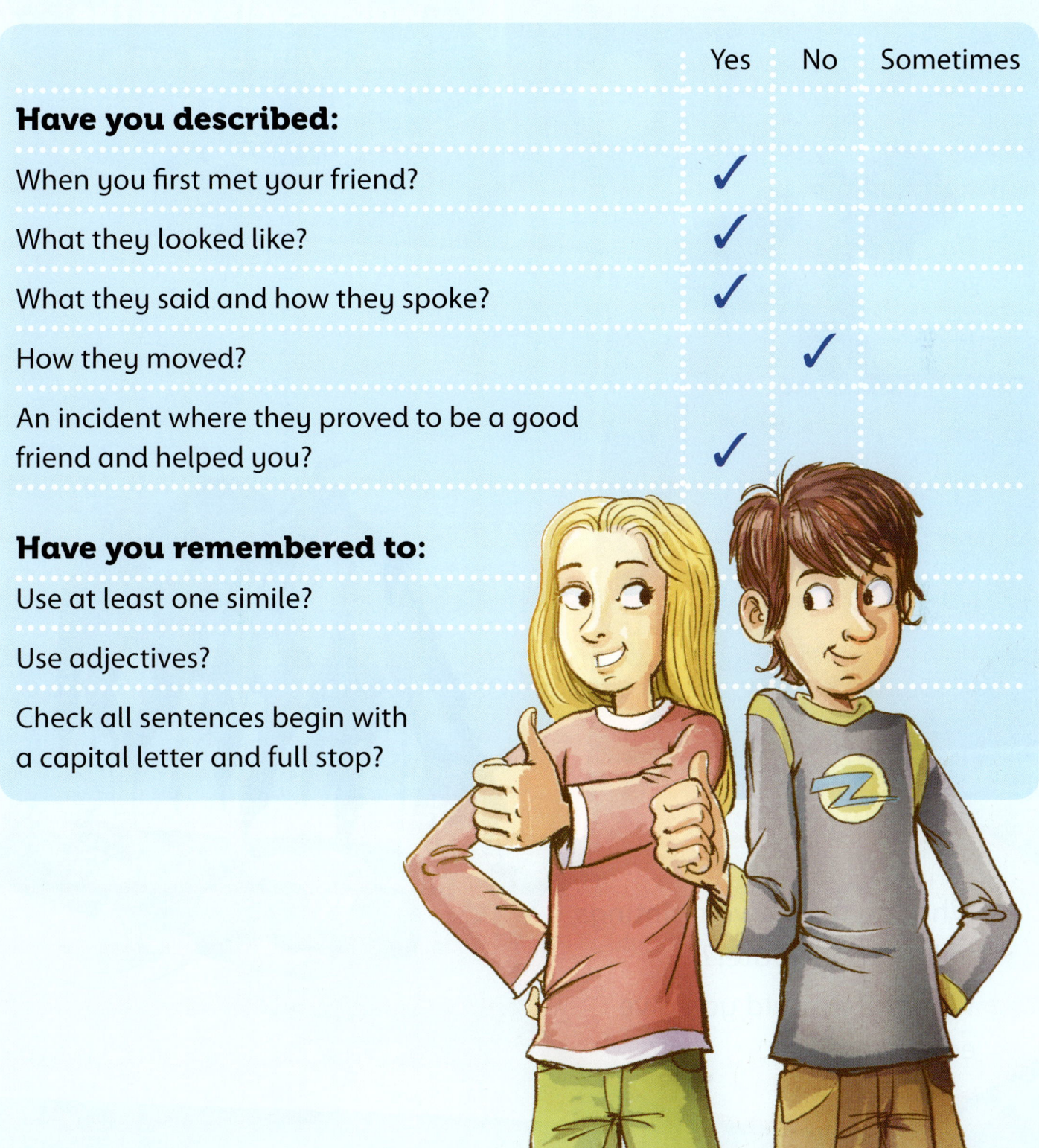

8 World of water

Non-Fiction Speaking and listening

"We forget that the water cycle and the life cycle are one."
Jacques Yves Cousteau

Let's Talk

1. What do these two paintings tell us about water?
2. What title would you give each painting?

Non-Fiction Speaking, listening and vocabulary

Words about water

Word Cloud
drench
oasis
well

 **A** **Look at the words in the Word Cloud and match them to the meanings here.**

1 A deep hole in the ground from which you can get water.
2 To soak someone or something with water.
3 A place in a desert where there is water.

 **B** Look at the brochure (right). How would you persuade your family to take you to this festival?

 **C** 22 March is World Water Day and schools all over the world organize events to help us remember the importance of water. What would you like your school to do on that day?

COME TO **THAILAND** and CELEBRATE NEW YEAR at the **WATER FESTIVAL**
Don't forget to bring a bucket of water or a water gun to drench your friends!

Non-Fiction Reading

Persuasive text

What We Can Do About Wasting Water

Water on Earth

Although there is so much water on Earth, most of it is salty and cannot be used for drinking. Only about 4 per cent is
5 fresh water…

A growing demand for water

We all need at least one litre of drinking water a day to keep us alive. We also use water for
10 washing ourselves, for washing our clothes and cars, to flush the toilet and to water our plants. In fact, every person uses about 140 litres of water a day. If we add the
15 water used by industry and farming, each person 'uses' about 600 litres of water a day…

Word Cloud
demand
supply
waste

Non-Fiction Reading

Avoiding waste
Imagine that the water supply to your house has been cut and you have to collect all the water you need from a well or standpipe. How would you use that water once you had carried it home?

Try to think how you and your family can avoid wasting water. For example, do not wash your hands or brush your teeth under a running tap. When you use a tap, make sure you turn it off properly. Dripping taps can waste a lot of water…

Saving water outside
People often leave hoses on for longer than is needed, and waste water. For many small gardens it is not really necessary to use a hose and sprinkler. Use a watering can instead. With a watering can you can make sure the water goes only where it is needed and none is wasted.

From *What We Can Do About Wasting Water*, by Donna Bailey

Glossary

industry
the business of making things, for example in factories

sprinkler
an object that sprays water

standpipe
a public water tap

Comprehension

Non-Fiction Comprehension

Read and answer the questions.

1. What percentage of the Earth's water can we use for drinking?
2. Why is this figure so low?
3. Name four different things we use water for.

Challenge
Design a poster or brochure to persuade people to use watering cans instead of using hoses or sprinklers.

What do you think?

1. Did the extract persuade you to use less water? Explain your answer.
2. Did you find any of the facts in the extract surprising? If so, which ones and why?
3. How would you feel if the water supply to your house was cut off? If this happened to you, would you use less water in the future?
4. Is the style of language used in this extract different to that in the tourist brochure on page 117? How would you describe the different styles?

Non-Fiction Comprehension

C What about you?

Do you think it is true that people in some countries are not careful with water? Discuss your ideas with a partner.

Discussion time

Sometimes water is responsible for causing serious problems. Do you think these situations can be avoided? Brainstorm ideas as a class.

Explanatory text

What Can You See in This Cloud?

Clouds

Clouds appear in many different forms. They can look like beautiful billowing masses of cotton wool in the sky. They can be the dark
5 messengers of coming storms. They can light up as fantastic lightning or crash and bang with noisy thunder…

Rain and water

Each type of cloud gives an idea of what sort
10 of weather to expect. Certain types bring rain, which provides vital water. Rain naturally waters the ground and allows plants to grow. Farmers need rain to grow crops for people and animals.

15 ### Trees

The biggest and most important plants in this cycle are trees… Trees produce filtered clean air, and help to form new clouds. Wind or heat causes excess rain water to evaporate so that
20 tiny droplets of water mingle with the air. In the right conditions the droplets come together and form clouds once again. They in turn will give the water back to the earth in the form of rain, continuing an everlasting cycle.

From *TreeTops: What Can You See in This Cloud?* by Matt Minshall

Word Cloud
billowing
evaporate
filtered
mingle

Comprehension

Non-Fiction Comprehension

Which sentence below is true?
1. All clouds look the same.
2. Crops need water to grow.
3. Trees cause rain water to evaporate.

What do you think?
1. Why do you think clouds are referred to as 'messengers' in the extract?
2. Water is described as 'vital' in the extract. What does this mean?
3. What is the importance of trees in the water cycle?
4. Choose one of the paragraphs in the extract. How would you summarize it in one sentence?

Discussion time
Imagine that there is a break in the water cycle. Why might this happen? Discuss the problems that occur when there is not enough water.

What about you?
Explain why the water cycle is called 'everlasting'. Draw a simple diagram to help with your explanation.

Connectives

Explanatory texts often use **connectives** such as **so** and **because** to show cause and effect and **time connectives** such as **then** and **after that**.

Persuasive texts often use connectives such as **if... so** and **if... then**, **although**, **however**, **therefore** and **because**.

Top Tip

Connectives are often used to help make an argument.

 **A** Copy out these sentences and underline the connectives.

1 There is a huge demand for water because there are so many people in the world.

2 However, some people don't think about the amount of water they waste.

3 If you run a tap, then make sure you turn it off afterwards.

 **B** Look at these connectives. Which three are time connectives?

although   firstly   and
afterwards   finally   because

Non-Fiction Grammar

 **Copy and complete these sentences using a connective.**

1. Water is precious _____ don't waste a drop! (so, nevertheless)
2. All the villagers use the well _____ it has clean water. (although, because)
3. Some people use a hose to clean the car. _____, they could use a bucket. (Because, However)
4. _____ your friends waste water, _____ persuade them not to! (If… then, Firstly… finally)

Challenge
Plan an advertisement for an imaginary water-saving product. How will you use connectives to persuade people to buy your product?

Non-Fiction Vocabulary

Words with common roots

A **root word** is a word that has meaning even with nothing added to it. It does not have a **prefix** or a **suffix**.

A root word can be used to create lots of different words. We can get clues about the meaning of different words by looking at the root word.

Example: comfort (root word)

    suffix   prefix   suffix
comfort**able** **un**comfort**able**

Top Tip

Remember: A **prefix** comes at the beginning of a word; a **suffix** comes at the end of the word. Prefixes and suffixes can alter the meaning of the words!

 **A** Copy and complete these bugs so that each leg has a word that comes from the root word in the centre.

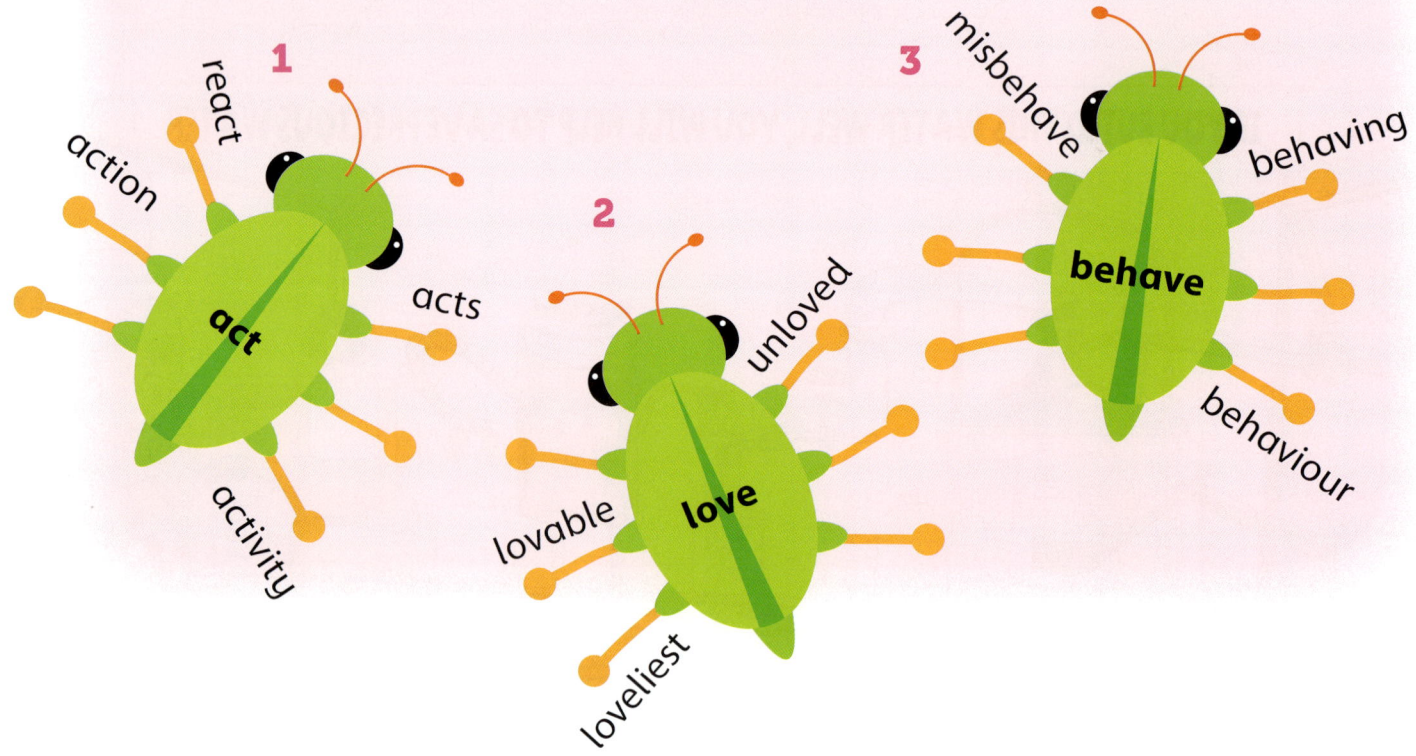

Non-Fiction Vocabulary

B Add a prefix, a suffix or both to the root word to make these sentences correct.

1. The women and girls are (carry) water from the well.
2. The class sang the new song (joy). Their parents (joy) the concert.
3. What an (grateful) child! He didn't thank the (help) man.

C A root is not always a complete word. Divide these words into four groups that have a common root.

medicine	telephone	biology	medical
portable	import	export	microphone
phonics	biography	medication	autobiography

Non-Fiction Writing workshop

Writing an explanatory text
Model writing

The water cycle
The water cycle is the journey water takes between the sea, the land and the sky.

1. Heat from the sun, together with the wind, causes water to evaporate and turn into water vapour (a gas).

2. Next, the water vapour rises to the sky. As it cools, it begins to form water droplets, which in turn form clouds.

3. Wind carries the clouds over the land and the water falls as rain or snow.

4. The rain runs off into streams and rivers, which flow into the sea. It also soaks through the soil. This water is called groundwater.

5. Then the warmth of the sun makes the water evaporate into water vapour and the cycle begins again.

water falls as rain or snow

winds

rising air

groundwater

Non-Fiction Writing workshop

Guided writing

An **explanatory text** is similar to a **non-chronological report**. For example, they both use more formal language. But there are some important differences!

A **non-chronological report** tells us how things are. It is usually organized by topic or theme.

An **explanatory text** explains a process or tells us how something works. It is organized in the order things happen.

Common features of an explanatory text

- Has an opening statement that tells the reader exactly what is going to be explained.
- May be presented in paragraphs, with each stage explained in a separate paragraph.
- May be presented as a flow chart, with each stage explained in a separate box.
- Often uses connectives to join ideas or time connectives.
- May include a labelled diagram.
- Explains difficult words.
- Has a conclusion.

Non-Fiction Writing workshop

Planning an explanatory text

Your writing

- Decide what your explanatory text is going to be about. The example on page 128 is about the water cycle, but you could write about something else, such as how to make bread or the life cycle of a butterfly.

- Research the process you are going to describe, writing down some key facts.

- Will you present your text in paragraphs or as a flow chart? If you choose paragraphs, make sure each paragraph has a subheading that makes it clear what the paragraph is going to be about.

- Will you need to include a diagram?

- Remember to explain any difficult words for the reader.

Even if you are going to write in paragraphs, you could make a flow chart first to organize your ideas.

Non-Fiction Writing workshop

Explanatory text success criteria

Before you write your text, draw a chart of success criteria, like the one below.

When you have written your text, share it with a partner. Which parts do they find less easy to understand? The test of a successful explanation is whether your reader understands it!

Together with your partner, fill in the chart you made. Can you improve your explanatory text?

	Yes	No	Sometimes
Begins with a general opening statement	✓		
Divides the stages up into paragraphs or boxes	✓		
Paragraphs have subheadings			✓
Each paragraph or box follows from the previous one			
Uses connectives to link ideas and time connectives			
Uses labelled diagrams or illustrations	✓		
Explains difficult words			
Has a conclusion	✓		

Poetry Speaking and listening

9 Poems for all seasons

"There is a way that nature speaks, that land speaks…"
Linda Hogan

Let's Talk

1. Describe how you think you would feel if you were high up in a hot air balloon or in the mountains on a snowboard.
2. Do you think our surroundings make a difference to how we feel? Explain your answer.

Poetry Speaking, listening and vocabulary

Words and syllables

Word Cloud
season
shape poem
syllable

 **Look at the words in the Word Cloud and match them to the meanings here.**

1 A word or part of a word with one vowel sound.
2 A poem in which the words are arranged in a special shape.
3 One of the four periods of the year: spring, summer, autumn and winter.

 **What do you notice about the number of syllables in this poem?**

This
is a
word journey
that started with
just one syllable
on the first lonely line,
but then increased to two, and
added one more with each new line
until the writer decided that
the journey's end should be at number ten.

Mike Jubb

 **Which is your favourite season? Think of words of one, two and three syllables to describe it. Share your words with a partner.**

133

Poetry Reading

Different forms of poems

Haiku

An old silent pond...
A frog jumps into the pond,
splash! Silence again.

Matsuo Basho, translated by Harry Behn

Tanka

Yellow Leaves

Yellow leaves falling
into the lake. Its surface
caressed by the breeze.

My thoughts hop from leaf to leaf
cleaving the breeze to the Sun.

Vassilis Comporozos

Cinquain

Snow

Look up...
From bleakening hills
Blows down the light, first breath
Of wintry wind...look up, and scent
The snow!

Adelaide Crapsey

Word Cloud
bleakening
caressed
cleaving
scent

Poetry Reading

Shape poem

Sun
Mary-Luz Espiritusanto

- Go to sleep, SUNSET.
- Wake up, SUNRISE.
- Summer fun, SUNLIGHT.
- Tell the time, SUNDIAL.
- Laugh and play, SUNSHINE.
- Summer plants, SUNFLOWER.
- Squint and blink, SUNBEAM.
- Sad and angry, SUNBURN.

Glossary

cinquain
a poem of five lines with the syllable pattern 2, 4, 6, 8, 2

haiku
a poem of three lines with the syllable pattern 5, 7, 5

tanka
a poem of five lines with the syllable pattern 5, 7, 5, 7, 7

Comprehension

Poetry Comprehension

 **Read and answer the questions.**

1 What topics do the different poems have in common?
2 Three of the poetry forms follow a particular syllable pattern. Which one does not?
3 Find an example of **alliteration** from one of the poems.
4 Find an example of **personification** from one of the poems.

Challenge
The haiku was written by Basho, a very famous Japanese poet. Do some research to find out more about him and read more of his haiku.

B What do you think?

1 How much time has passed from the start of the shape poem to the end?
2 Which words or phrases in the poems did you find most effective?
3 Did you dislike any of the poems? Give reasons for your answer.

Discussion time
Many poets are inspired by nature and the changing of the seasons. What do you find inspiring in nature? Share your ideas in a small group.

Poetry Comprehension

C What about you?

Get some inspiration for a nature poem of your own! Choose one of the places below and one of the seasons. Imagine you are in that place in that season. What can you see, smell and feel? Write five descriptive words that come into your mind.

- On a beach
- At the top of a hill
- In a woodland
- Beside a river
- In the mountains
- In the desert

- Spring
- Summer
- Autumn
- Winter

Poetry Reading

Different forms of poems (continued)

List poem

Spring is in the Air

spring cleaning,
spring planting,
spring pruning,

bees,
butterflies,
allergies,

campfires,
marshmallows,
smores*,

spring break,
school is out soon,
happy tired children,

the smell of flowers,
fresh spring rain,
first mowed grass,

just a few of my favorite** things!

Karen Croft

*Smores are roasted marshmallows.
**'Favorite' is the US spelling of 'favourite'.

Limerick

There was an Old Man in a Tree

There was an Old Man in a tree,
Who was horribly bored by a bee;
When they said, "Does it buzz?"
He replied, "Yes, it does!"
"It's a regular brute of a bee!"

Edward Lear

Word Cloud
allergies
brute
dale
vale

Riddle

My first is in water, but isn't in air,

My second's in ocean and sea, but not there.

My third's in a river but not in a vale,

My fourth is in stream, but not moor, hill or dale.

My fifth can be seen in a ditch – not a street –

And my whole can be found under everyone's feet.

Alison Chisholm

Glossary

list poem
a poem that uses a list structure

limerick
a funny poem of five lines

riddle poem
a puzzle set out as a poem

Comprehension

Poetry Comprehension

A **Which sentence below is true?**
1. A limerick has no rhyme or rhythm.
2. A list poem has to rhyme.
3. A riddle poem is a like a puzzle that you have to work out.

Challenge
'My whole' in the riddle poem is the answer. Can you work it out? (Clue: 'My first' means the first letter of the answer, 'my second' means the second letter, and so on.)

B **What do you think?**
1. Which pairs of words in the riddle poem rhyme?
2. Do you think a list poem has a pattern or structure? Explain your answer.
3. Which of the three poems did you like the most and why?

C **What about you?**
The poem 'Spring is in the Air' lists things that make the poet think of spring. Compare the poet's images of spring with spring in the country you live in. What is different and what is the same? Discuss your ideas with a partner.

Poetry Grammar and vocabulary

Same letters, different sound

Some words contain the same letters in the same order, but we pronounce the words differently. Look at these words, which all contain the letter string **ear**.

l**ear**n

b**ear**

ear

h**ear**t

Say the words aloud. What do you notice?

A Sort these words into four groups that have the same sound.

wear	fear	bear
year	earn	heartbeat
early	kindhearted	heard
beard	pear	hearth

140

Poetry Grammar and vocabulary

 Which word in the cloud has the same sound as the word in the sun?

tough
cough rough
through

rice
police nice
practice

shout
journey four
without

 Which words with the **oo** string complete this rhyming poem?

If I'm the m**oo**d

to eat some nice ____.

I look in a b**oo**k

and ch**oo**se what to ____!

Challenge
Think of four more words with the **oo** string – two with the **oo** sound in 'mood' and two with the **oo** sound in 'book'.

141

Poetry Writing workshop

Model poems

Tanka

Wind rustles gently
In almost bare trees, waiting.
The sky threatens rain
Then a quick burst of sunlight
And a rising skylark sings.

Haiku

The long school day ends
Children scatter like litter
Happy to be free.

Cinquain

Cold rain
Falling fiercely
We are like stranded fish
Splashing through wet,
  grey streets swimming
For home

Poetry Writing workshop

Guided writing

Remember: A **tanka** has the syllable pattern 5, 7, 5, 7, 7.
A **cinquain** has the syllable pattern 2, 4, 6, 8, 2.
A **haiku** has the syllable pattern 5, 7, 5.

Choose the type of poem you like best. Copy it out so that you draw lines between each syllable of each word. This should look like this: 'wait/ing'. Count the number of syllables in each line. Do they match the syllable pattern of the poem?

Top Tip
Count the syllables as you are writing, saying the words out loud.

Writing your own poem

Now it is your turn to write a poem. Here are some subjects you could write about:

- The seasons: summer, winter, spring, autumn
- The weather: rain, snow, wind, fog, heat
- Feelings: sadness, love, hope, fear
- People: friend, grandparent, sister, father

Read your poem out loud to a partner. Do they agree with your syllable count for each line? Which line of the poem did they like best, and why?

Revise and check 3

Units 7, 8 and 9

Vocabulary

1 Complete the sentences with these words:

waste oasis syllables tumbling

a The leaves came _____ down.
b How many _____ in a haiku poem?
c Don't _____ water!
d Look, an _____ at last!

whooshed well demand drenched

e Oh no, Anna, you're _____!
f The wind _____ across the hills.
g Is there a growing _____ for water?
h Keep away from the _____!

Punctuation

1 Look at the sentences in the vocabulary exercises above.
a Which of the sentences are questions?
b Which of the sentences are statements?
c Which of the sentences are exclamations?
d Which of the sentences are commands?

Describe the different punctuation that is needed for each type of sentence.

Units 7, 8 and 9

Grammar

1 Divide the words below into families and write them in columns with the root word at the top.

agreed   unhelpful   clearing
helping   cleared   helps
disagree   unclear   agreement

Help   Clear   Agree

2 Find the connectives in this word snake and write a list.

thenafterwardsfirstlyfinallybecauseandnext

3 Use some of the connectives in the word snake above to join these sentences.

a Check your local weather report. Make sure there is enough wind!

b Find a large open area. Hold the kite in both hands. Toss it into the wind.

c Keep an eye on your kite. Sometimes the wind changes and the kite can crash.

d Bring the kite down. Slowly wind the kite string around a spool.

Spelling

1 Copy out the sentences below using the correct word.

a Granny came to stay for a (**weak week**).

b They carried the sack of (**flour flower**) into the kitchen.

c Meet me under the (**pear pair**) tree!

d The boy (**blue blew**) out all the candles on the cake.

e Don't forget to (**weight wait**) for your sister!

Carving the Sea Path

Chapter One

Irniq watched the massive shadow weave its way under the thick ice. His almond eyes grew dark.

He slumped down onto the hard, white sea and rubbed the smooth, glassy surface. The ice was dense and thick, yet Irniq could see something below.

He squinted, searching down into the deep. His heart missed a beat. Yes, it was there, slowly rolling beneath him like a mighty black wave. The shadow coasted under Irniq's tense, crouching body for what seemed a lifetime, then its mighty tail fin flipped and disappeared into the depths.

Fiction Reading

Irniq looked across the frozen winter sea.
15 It seemed as if winter had come so quickly. Summer had faded, just like his special friendship with Samuel.

Irniq thought back to the summer months when sandpipers, dunlins and orange-beaked
20 king eiders came flying in to graze for the season. He'd watched the grand arrival of blue, minke, humpback and grey whales. They coasted west, following leads through icy sea paths to feed in richer waters.

25 His heart had pounded as he watched mighty humpbacks breaching. He'd held his breath and imagined the whole sea emptying onto the shore as the whales landed with a thundering crash onto the surface, sending shock waves
30 and froth up into the sky.

Chapter Two

"I think they're crazy," Samuel said to him, one warm summer's day.

Samuel was a new boy at school and hadn't wanted to come to the Arctic. His father was a researcher posted in the town for a year.

Samuel was always angry. Mainly with his father for moving him here. Samuel hated it – the cold and the quiet. He never joined in school clubs and spent every break alone, playing on his games console.

The other children left Samuel alone. He didn't seem interested in them, so they weren't interested in him.

"After all," Samuel continued moaning to Irniq, "who or what would want to come here? Who would leave the Californian coast or the steaming hot beaches of Mexico for this freezing dump? Whales are mad."

Irniq felt insulted, yet at the same time, there
50 was something he liked about Samuel.

  Irniq wondered how he would have felt if he'd been wrenched from his beautiful Arctic home to live in a high-rise block in a strange, smoggy city. He shivered at the thought.

55 "Do you know those crazy fish swim 12,400 miles a year, North to South, South to North? Or so Dad told me," scoffed Samuel.

  "They're not fish, they're mammals," Irniq said, beginning to feel irritated.

60 "They all look the same to me," said Samuel, bored.

  "Is your dad on the boat today?" asked Irniq.

  He'd often watched and envied Samuel's dad tracking the whales in the research boat.

65 "Sure is. Where else would he be? Not with me, that's for sure," said Samuel resentfully. "No, he's out counting those crazy fish over and over again."

70 "Why don't you go out with him?" said Irniq. "You never know, you might like it."

"Are you kidding? I'd puke. Anyway, once you've seen one 75 crazy fish, you've seen them all," said Samuel.

Irniq had had enough of Samuel's whinging, so he turned and walked homewards.

80 "Hey, Irney, want to come and play on the computer?" Samuel called, running after him.

"I keep telling you, my name's Irniq, not Irney," snapped Irniq.

"Sure, sorry. How about it then? I'm on level 85 13." Samuel's eyes lit up as he spoke.

Irniq knew that Samuel must be lonely, but if he'd just stop moaning, then maybe the other kids wouldn't avoid him so much.

90 Irniq smiled, "OK. Go on then."

Chapter Three

Irniq couldn't believe the amazing things Samuel had in his home.

Samuel's kitchen was filled with gadgets that bleeped, squeaked and sent out frothy milkshakes and hot popcorn within seconds.

"Guilt," said Samuel, winking. "It comes in handy." He passed Irniq some popcorn.

Samuel's mum was in the living room watching a TV that looked bigger than Irniq's kitchen table, and when they moved on to Samuel's room, it was even more impressive.

"Wow! You've got some amazing games," Irniq said in awe, inspecting Samuel's CD stand, which was almost as tall as him.

"Yep, every game title," Samuel said proudly.

Irniq was happy to go and play at Samuel's every evening. He discovered to his surprise, that he and Samuel had the same sense of humour and they liked the same things. Not only that, they were at about the same level in most things at school, except for Irniq's great knowledge of Arctic wildlife.

But as the days passed, Irniq began to miss being outside with his friends. He wanted Samuel to meet them all, play outside with the
125 group and make the most of the last days of summer. But Samuel wasn't interested.

Whatever Irniq suggested, Samuel just said, "Maybe tomorrow," in his usual bored tone.

"Let's go out and play football or
130 basketball," Irniq said to Samuel one day. "There's a special area where everyone goes, it's great, there's hoops and all."

"You've got to be kidding, it's freezing," Samuel scoffed.

135 "It's summer. When you're running around you don't notice the cold," Irniq said.

"No way," said Samuel. "I hate this place."

"We always do what you want to do. Come out and play football," said Irniq. "Please."

Irniq had already missed out on kayaking and cycling with his mates. He was beginning to worry that by playing only with Samuel he'd lose his other friends.

But Samuel wouldn't budge.

"I'm not coming out," he snapped angrily. "Just leave it."

Irniq slung on his parker and shrugged, "I'm going then," he said, defeated.

Samuel ignored Irniq, and was so engrossed in his computer game that he didn't notice when Irniq marched out of the room.

The next day, Irniq swallowed his pride and called on Samuel again. But Samuel still refused to come out.

Chapter Four

After a while Irniq gave up on Samuel and spent the rest of his time catching up on summer sports with his friends. He knew summer was precious and not to be missed. But he missed Samuel's unique sense of humour and special friendship, too.

Sometimes he'd see Samuel wandering back from the stores carrying a comic. Samuel seemed to look through him and never smiled; it upset Irniq.

Then Irniq heard the first sounds of winter howling in on freezing winds. He watched his favourite summer visitors flee to escape the winter's cold. Summer birds gathered themselves into chaotic flocks, hooting and calling to warn each other of the impending freeze.

And as the summer came to an end, Irniq and Samuel's friendship became a distant memory…

Now it was deep winter and, as Irniq crouched in the silence of the frozen sea, he became more and more convinced that a grey whale was trapped, helpless in the closing ice.

If it stayed there, it would die.

But how could he rescue it?

"Looking for treasure?" Samuel's voice startled Irniq.

Irniq quickly looked round.

Samuel was standing a few yards away, shivering miserably and wiping his streaming nose.

"I thought you'd be here," Samuel snuffled hesitantly. "You said it was special."

"It's my favourite place," Irniq replied, looking up at the sky. "It's like this for weeks.

The sky just stays on fire, like magic."

Samuel smiled, yet he looked sad.

"Do you want a game of football?" Samuel said sheepishly.

Irniq's eyes lit up. But suddenly he remembered the trapped whale.

"No, I can't," said Irniq quickly.

"Oh, OK," Samuel said, shuffling disappointedly. He turned to go.

"I've found a trapped whale," Irniq suddenly blurted out.

"Where?" said Samuel, his eyes lighting up.

"Right here," replied Irniq, pointing down to the ice.

Samuel hunched next to Irniq and gazed downwards.

"It's just waves," said Samuel, his warm breath bouncing off the ice.

"No, look," Irniq said urgently.

The two boys crouched silently together, watching until…

"There! Look!" Irniq shouted triumphantly.

215 The great whale's body darkened the ice beneath them.

"Wow," Samuel chuckled. "Maybe it's a submarine. Maybe it's a spy sub…"

Irniq grinned and shook his head. "No, it's
220 a grey whale. Look at the way its shadow moves and bends. I just can't understand why it hasn't migrated."

"I know," said Samuel. "I heard Dad telling someone that the whales are staying later each
225 year because there's not enough food for them to eat before migration. They can't migrate if they are hungry."

"What are we going to do?" said Irniq. "It's going to die."

230 "Come on," Samuel yanked Irniq's sleeve excitedly. "Dad will know."

Chapter Five

The boys ran back to town. Samuel's dad was in his office.

"Dad, Irniq's found a stranded whale," Samuel said breathlessly.

"Where?" asked his dad.

"At his favourite place," Samuel replied.

His dad smiled. "How would I know where that is, Sam?" he laughed.

"Come on, I'll show you," said Irniq.

Samuel's dad leapt up and grabbed his kit. "Lead the way," he said, and Samuel and Irniq raced to the door, eager to lead him to the trapped whale.

Word spread quickly and, within a few hours, the whole village was marching out across the ice, armed with anything that would break through its solid thick surface.

Samuel's dad had also gathered a workforce from his offices. "We're going to have to carve a path out of the frozen ice for the whale," he shouted to everyone, "or it will die."

Irniq and Samuel stood proudly beside him as the researchers and the villagers all set to work.

That was the start of their wonderful adventure.

Chapter Six

For the next four weeks, Samuel and Irniq watched snowmobiles and dog sleds scooting madly around. Scientists and villagers worked around the clock, drilling and cutting out massive patches of ice.

Each time a new air hole was made, the work crews cheered and commenced work on the next one, creating a channel that went further and further out towards the open sea, leading the trapped whale to safety.

Then, one day, as Samuel and Irniq stood beside an air hole they watched a rising shadow through the ice.

Suddenly up through the water burst the mighty head of the grey whale.

Samuel shrieked with shock and delight.

Irniq calmly knelt down.

"She's come to thank you," Samuel's dad shouted to them.

280 Irniq slowly reached out his hand and gently he touched the tip of the whale's ice-cold nose.

Samuel gasped and knelt. Tentatively he touched the whale's great head. His eyes grew wide in wonder, "She's beautiful," he exclaimed.

285 Irniq smiled.

"Quyanaq," Irniq said proudly to the whale as it descended majestically back into the depths.

"Quyanaq," said Samuel, trying out his very first word in Inupiat. "Thank you."

290 It had taken a long time, but Samuel had finally realised that he had a very special friend in Irniq, and for the first time in all the months he had lived there, he felt at home in the Arctic and a part of everything around him.

Carving the Sea Path by Kathryn White

Fiction Reading

Word Cloud
Arctic
Inupiat
migration
tentatively
unique
wrenched